SuperHabits
For Success

The Secrets to Lasting Habit Change Using
Modern Science & Ancient Wisdom in 3 Easy Steps

Dr. Tony Nader, MD, PhD, Robert Keith Wallace, PhD,
Miriam Claes Lodge, MS, IR, Heathere Evans, MA, Ted Wallace, MS

To our very dear children and grandchildren

CONTENTS

INTRODUCTION

WHY SUPERHABITS?

I came to the program wanting to start exercising. I've been trying to do that for 20 years. I got gym memberships, I got treadmills, I subscribed to various programs, but I think what was missing for me was the how: how to take this desire and make it into a habit, something I would do every day. It's two months after the program and I'm sticking to it and I'm exercising daily – so it works.

– Seema Kashyap, SuperHabits program participant

Despite the wealth of information on habit change, many people still find it challenging to create lasting improvements in their lives. This is unfortunate, as simple lifestyle changes can lead to significant improvements in happiness, health, and overall well-being. Most health experts agree that embracing habits in four main areas—diet, exercise, sleep, and stress management—can dramatically improve our quality of life. Studies have consistently demonstrated that these habits are associated with increased longevity, reduced risk of chronic diseases, better mental health, and even improved cognitive function.

Yet, despite the clear benefits, why don't more people succeed in making these changes permanent?

The reality is that habit change is not a linear process; it's deeply complex and multi-dimensional. It's often hindered by limiting attitudes such as self-doubt, procrastination, anxiety, and fear of failure. Beyond these visible barriers lie deeply embedded subconscious beliefs and emotional triggers that have a powerful influence on behavior. These hidden mental patterns, developed over years, act like an invisible operating system that directs our actions and decisions—often without our conscious awareness. This is why many people find themselves reverting to old habits, despite knowing what they "should" be doing.

In this book, we will explore a unique, consciousness-based approach to habit change called the SuperHabits approach. This approach delves into deeper levels of the mind, helping to rewire neural pathways for the easier adoption of new habits. We also offer the SuperHabits program, which is a 10-week online group coaching program. Participants have shown remarkable results, with 94% reporting significant progress in their target habits and 95% recommending the program to others. These results suggest that a consciousness-based approach can be a powerful tool, even for those who have struggled with habit change in the past.

Olivia's Story: A struggle with habits

To illustrate how the SuperHabits approach works, let's consider the story of Olivia, a 35-year-old entrepreneur navigating the challenges of running a rapidly growing tech startup. Olivia's business success was evident—her company was thriving, and she was respected as a leader in her industry. However, behind this professional facade was a different story. Olivia felt a constant undercurrent of stress, fatigue, and a sense of being overwhelmed. Her days were packed with meetings, deadlines, and decision-making, leaving little time for personal well-being. Quick, unhealthy meals were the norm, and exercise was rare, usually squeezed into her schedule sporadically and inconsistently.

Despite knowing that better habits could improve her energy, mood, and productivity, Olivia found it nearly impossible to implement changes that lasted more than a few weeks. Her attempts were often followed by a sense of failure, as her old habits would inevitably resurface. This cycle of trying and failing not only drained her motivation but also reinforced negative beliefs about her abilities. Olivia began to believe she lacked the discipline necessary for lasting change, viewing herself as someone who simply "wasn't built" to maintain a healthy lifestyle. This internal narrative only deepened her resistance to trying new strategies.

Olivia's story is emblematic of what many people experience. It highlights a core problem: knowledge alone is rarely sufficient to drive lasting behavior change. The issue is not a lack of information or awareness, but rather the presence of underlying subconscious barriers that create resistance. The key to overcoming these barriers lies in addressing the deeper levels of the mind where these patterns are stored and maintained.

The Three Core Elements of the SuperHabits Approach

The SuperHabits approach is designed around three essential elements, represented as concentric circles in a diagram:

1. *Awareness* (Innermost circle): This element focuses on developing self-awareness and understanding one's personal mind-body type, based on the principles of Ayurveda.

2. *Consciousness* (Middle circle): This section emphasizes using consciousness-based techniques to access deeper levels of the mind, helping to overcome internal resistance.

3. *Toolkit* (Outer circle): This section provides practical tools for creating and maintaining new habits, including various coaching strategies, motivational techniques, and environmental design.

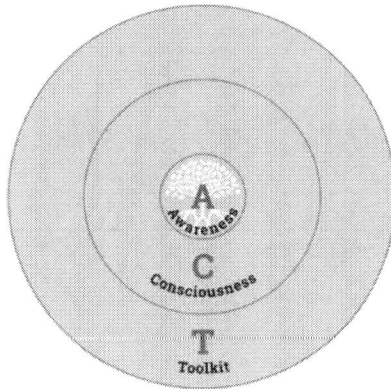

These three elements can be easily remembered by the acronym *ACT*: *Awareness*, *Consciousness*, and *Toolkit*. Let's break down each of these elements in detail and explore how they contribute to lasting habit change.

Awareness: The Foundation of Habit Change

The first step in the SuperHabits approach is awareness, understanding who you are, what motivates you, and how you respond to stress, change, and challenges. Research in psychology shows that self-awareness is one of the most critical factors for personal growth and behavior change. It allows individuals to understand their internal triggers, recognize patterns, and develop strategies tailored to their unique needs. This level of awareness is essential for designing a habit-change plan that works in the long term, as it accounts for individual differences rather than assuming a one-size-fits-all approach.

In the SuperHabits approach, the ancient system of Ayurveda is used as a framework to enhance self-awareness. Ayurveda, a 5,000-year-old holistic health system from India, identifies different mind-body types, or doshas—Vata, Pitta, and Kapha— that influence both mental and physical characteristics. These doshas are not just physical constitutions; they also reveal mental tendencies, emotional responses, and stress resilience.

For Olivia, understanding her Pitta nature was a breakthrough. Pittas are driven, ambitious, and goal-oriented, traits that often contribute to success in business and leadership. However, they can also become impatient, critical, and prone to burnout when they don't manage stress effectively. This realization helped Olivia reframe her struggles not as personal failures, but as natural tendencies that needed to be managed. She learned that her intense drive, while beneficial in many areas of life, could also lead to imbalance if not aligned with supportive habits.

Olivia's new awareness enabled her to make specific adjustments that were aligned with her Pitta nature. For example, she began incorporating more cooling foods into her diet, practicing calming breathing exercises, and engaging in evening rituals to promote relaxation. Ayurveda also emphasizes the importance of daily routines, or dinacharya, which are designed to create balance throughout the day. For Olivia, this meant adopting small, consistent habits, such as starting her morning with a glass of warm water and incorporating 10-minute breaks into her workday for mindful breathing. These changes may seem small, but they had a cumulative effect on Olivia's energy, mood, and stress levels.

Consciousness: Accessing Deeper Levels of the Mind

The second element of the SuperHabits approach is consciousness. This aspect is what truly sets this approach apart from all the other habit change methods, as it involves accessing deeper levels of the mind to facilitate change. Neuroscience has shown that our brain's neural pathways are shaped by both conscious thoughts and subconscious beliefs. While the conscious mind is responsible for immediate decision-making, the subconscious mind stores deeper patterns, beliefs, and memories that significantly influence behavior. Effective habit change requires engaging both levels of the mind, particularly the subconscious, which is where most behavioral resistance resides.

To illustrate the concept of consciousness, imagine the mind as an ocean. On the surface, the waves represent the conscious mind, filled with thoughts, worries, and distractions. As we go deeper, the water becomes calmer, representing the subconscious mind, which stores deeper beliefs, habits, and emotions. At the very bottom lies a state of pure consciousness, which is characterized by clarity, calmness, and creativity. It is at this level that true transformation can occur, as it allows individuals to access and release subconscious barriers that typically sabotage habit change.

The SuperHabits approach uses several consciousness-based techniques to help participants access this deeper state. One of the most powerful tools is Transcendental Meditation (TM), a simple, effortless technique that has been extensively researched for its effects on reducing stress, enhancing creativity, and improving mental clarity.

Olivia's experience with TM was transformative. Initially, she was skeptical about the effectiveness of meditation, but she committed to practicing TM for 20 minutes twice a day. Within just a few weeks, she noticed significant changes. Her mind felt clearer, she was less reactive to stressful situations, and her decision-making improved. TM provided a mental reset, allowing Olivia to approach her goals with a sense of calm and confidence rather than anxiety.

The SuperHabits approach also includes other consciousness-based tools, such as breathing exercises, yoga, aromatherapy, and lifestyle changes. For instance, Olivia learned a breathing exercise called pranayama, which she found particularly helpful during stressful moments at work. This simple technique helped her quickly calm her nervous system, regain focus, and make better decisions. Aromatherapy, another tool in the approach, helped Olivia calm her fiery Pitta nature so it was easier for her to adopt new habits. She made other lifestyle changes that helped her live a balanced, healthy lifestyle, which strengthened her motivation and sense of possibility.

Toolkit: Practical Strategies for Lasting Change

The final component of the SuperHabits approach is the Toolkit, a set of practical strategies for creating and maintaining habits. The Toolkit includes a variety of tools designed to support motivation, track progress, and provide feedback. These tools are organized into four main categories:

Self-Coaching

Techniques such as journaling, habit tracking, and inner inquiry help participants develop greater self-awareness and accountability. Olivia found that keeping a daily habit journal was one of the most effective tools for maintaining her new habits. In her journal, she tracked her daily progress, reflected on successes and challenges, and set intentions for the next day. This process not only kept her accountable but also provided insights into what was working and what needed adjustment.

Partner Coaching

In the SuperHabits 10-week program, participants are paired with a partner, providing mutual support and accountability. Olivia's partner, Ethan, became an essential part of her journey. Their daily text messages and weekly check-ins helped her stay motivated and provided a sense of camaraderie. They shared successes, discussed challenges, and encouraged each other during tough moments. Having an accountability partner added a layer of psychological support that helped Olivia maintain momentum. Even if you are not enrolled in the structured SuperHabits program, we still recommend you try to organize an accountability partner from your personal network.

Group Coaching

Each of the 10 live, online meetings of the SuperHabits program, includes a small group discussion called a learning circle. These learning circles offer collective growth and peer mentorship. These small group sessions create a supportive environment where participants can share insights, discuss challenges, and learn from each other. For Olivia, the learning circles were a highlight of the program. She found inspiration in hearing others' stories, which helped her realize that setbacks were a natural part of the process and not a personal failure.

Environmental Coaching

The approach encourages participants to optimize their surroundings to support desired habits. This can include rearranging their home or workspace, creating a dedicated meditation or exercise area, or keeping healthy snacks within reach. Olivia made several adjustments, such as setting up a quiet meditation space in her living room, placing reminders for hydration at her desk, and keeping a yoga mat in her office for quick stretches.

Key Principles

The SuperHabits approach emphasizes several principles.

- Start small: Begin with an easy-to-do habit to reduce resistance. Olivia started with a five-minute meditation, which gradually increased as she gained confidence.

- Use affirmations: Encourage a positive frame of mind. Olivia used affirmations such as "I am capable of change" and "I am committed to my well-being," which helped shift her mindset from doubt to empowerment.

- Adapt and learn: Treat each setback as a learning opportunity. When Olivia missed a workout, she analyzed what went wrong and adjusted her approach accordingly.

- Emphasize progress, not perfection: Consistency is more important than perfection. Olivia focused on celebrating small victories, such as choosing a healthier meal or taking a short walk, which kept her motivated.

- Avoid anxiety about results: Focus on steady progress rather than immediate success. Olivia learned to appreciate the process of change, which made it more sustainable and enjoyable.

Conclusion: The Power of Consciousness-Based Habit Change

The SuperHabits approach offers a transformative path to lasting habit change by addressing the deeper layers of the mind. By integrating awareness, consciousness-based techniques, and a comprehensive Toolkit, the approach provides a holistic approach to adopting new habits. For Olivia, this approach was the missing piece she had been searching for. Instead of feeling trapped by her old patterns, she experienced a newfound sense of freedom and confidence. She not only established healthier habits but also developed a more compassionate relationship with herself, making it easier to maintain these changes over time.

The journey toward lasting habit change may require patience and persistence, but the rewards—improved health, happiness, and quality of life—are well worth the effort. By embracing the principles of Awareness, Consciousness, and the Toolkit, individuals can break free from limiting patterns and create lasting, positive change.

SECTION 1

AWARENESS

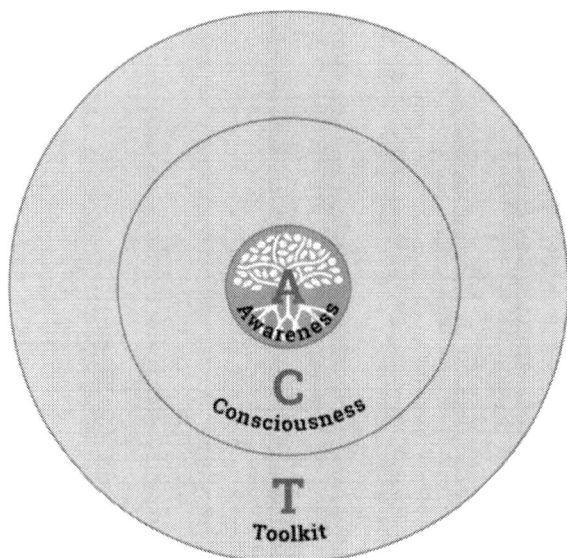

CHAPTER 1

AWARENESS

Whatever we put our attention on
will grow stronger in our life.

– Maharishi Mahesh Yogi

We are all different. Some people learn more quickly than others. Some have lots of energy, others excel as athletes or artists. Some people live longer, and some face health challenges earlier in life. The same variety applies to adopting new habits: some people adopt them quickly, while others take longer; some maintain new habits for years, while others drop out within weeks. We all have a mix of good and bad habits, and the first step in making positive changes is to become aware of who we truly are.

Have you ever heard the phrase "nature versus nurture"? This single concept explains much about human behavior and personality. It suggests that we are shaped by both the genes we inherit (nature) and the environment we grow up and live in (nurture). While we can't change the genes we were born with, we can influence how they express themselves.

Our genes don't operate in isolation—the field of epigenetics explains how genes can be activated and deactivated based on external factors like diet, relationships, stress, climate, and even our thoughts and emotions.

Why Personalization is Key to Habit Change

The nature-versus-nurture framework highlights why habit change must be personalized. There is no universal strategy that works for everyone, because each individual is shaped by a unique blend of genetic traits and life experiences. While there are key principles that apply to most people, a truly effective habit change approach needs to be tailored to individual differences. But how do we personalize such an approach? Some approaches focus on preferred learning styles, personality profiles, career dynamics, or cultural background. In the SuperHabits approach, we take a unique angle rooted in ancient wisdom, yet supported by modern science.

Our method draws from Ayurveda, the holistic healthcare originating from India. While many people associate Ayurveda with massages or herbal teas, it is much more than that. Ayurveda is a comprehensive approach to health, emphasizing balance in mind and body. It complements Western medicine, especially because of its prevention-oriented nature. Today, modern science increasingly validates the principles of Ayurveda, recognizing its value in enhancing well-being and preventing disease.

Ayurveda's core philosophy is to create balance by understanding each individual's unique mind-body type. This is especially valuable in habit change because it explains why some people adopt new habits easily while others struggle. According to Ayurveda, every individual is born with a specific combination of three doshas—Vata, Pitta, and Kapha. Let's take a brief quiz to get an idea of your mind/body as this will be a foundation for the rest of the approach.

Mind-Body State Quiz

VATA MIND-BODY STATE	*STRONGLY DISAGREE / STRONGLY AGREE*				
1. Light sleeper, difficulty falling asleep	[1]	[2]	[3]	[4]	[5]
2. Irregular appetite	[1]	[2]	[3]	[4]	[5]
3. Learns quickly but forgets quickly	[1]	[2]	[3]	[4]	[5]
4. Easily becomes overstimulated	[1]	[2]	[3]	[4]	[5]
5. Does not tolerate cold weather very well	[1]	[2]	[3]	[4]	[5]
6. A sprinter rather than a marathoner	[1]	[2]	[3]	[4]	[5]
7. Speech is energetic, with frequent changes in topic	[1]	[2]	[3]	[4]	[5]
8. Anxious and worried when under stress	[1]	[2]	[3]	[4]	[5]
VATA SCORE	*(Total your responses)*				

◯ *PITTA MIND-BODY STATE*	*STRONGLY DISAGREE / STRONGLY AGREE*				
1. Easily becomes overheated	[1]	[2]	[3]	[4]	[5]
2. Strong reaction when challenged	[1]	[2]	[3]	[4]	[5]
3. Uncomfortable when meals are delayed	[1]	[2]	[3]	[4]	[5]
4. Good at physical activity	[1]	[2]	[3]	[4]	[5]
5. Strong appetite	[1]	[2]	[3]	[4]	[5]
6. Good sleeper but may not need as much sleep as others	[1]	[2]	[3]	[4]	[5]
7. Clear and precise speech	[1]	[2]	[3]	[4]	[5]
8. Becomes irritable and/or angry under stress	[1]	[2]	[3]	[4]	[5]
PITTA SCORE	*(Total your responses)*				

KAPHA MIND-BODY STATE	STRONGLY DISAGREE / STRONGLY AGREE				
1. Slow eater	[1]	[2]	[3]	[4]	[5]
2. Falls asleep easily but wakes up slowly	[1]	[2]	[3]	[4]	[5]
3. Steady, stable temperament	[1]	[2]	[3]	[4]	[5]
4. Doesn't mind waiting to eat	[1]	[2]	[3]	[4]	[5]
5. Slow to learn but rarely forgets	[1]	[2]	[3]	[4]	[5]
6. Good physical strength and stamina	[1]	[2]	[3]	[4]	[5]
7. Speech may be slow and thoughtful	[1]	[2]	[3]	[4]	[5]
8. Possessive and stubborn under stress	[1]	[2]	[3]	[4]	[5]
KAPHA SCORE	(Total your responses)				

Compare all three scores. Whichever total is higher, Vata, Pitta, or Kapha, is your primary mind-body type. It is common to have two high scores and one lower score. This shows that you are a combination of two main types, with a minor influence from the third. In some cases, you may have three similar scores. This is somewhat rare and indicates that you are a

Tri-type. You may also find that your score highlights one primary mind-body type. This means that every aspect of your life is strongly influenced by this type.

The key point to understand here is that no Ayurvedic combination (Vata, Pitta, Kapha) is superior to any others. Whether you have a Pitta-Kapha constitution or any other combination, you are wonderful in your own way. Each combination contributes to the whole and is equally important. Individuals are born with a specific combination, but it may change throughout their lives. It's similar to our DNA, which remains constant, yet different genes are expressed at different times in life. According to Ayurveda there is also a change in the influence of each dosha with aging. Even more important is the idea that certain behaviors can cause our mind-body type to become imbalanced. Understanding your Ayurvedic mind-body type and how it becomes out of balance will enable you to improve not only your ability to adopt new habits but every aspect of your life.

Sophia's Journey to Awareness: Embracing her Vata nature

Sophia, a 42-year-old graphic designer, was renowned for her creativity and spontaneity. Her passion for art led her to a successful career, but this same spontaneous nature made maintaining routines a constant struggle. Over the years, Sophia had tried different habit-change programs to establish healthier habits, such as regular exercise and meditation.

However, each attempt ended the same way: with excitement at the start, followed by boredom and eventual abandonment.

Sophia's struggle was familiar to many—a cycle of enthusiasm, followed by disappointment and self-blame. She blamed herself for lacking discipline and wondered why she couldn't sustain habits that seemed so easy for others. It wasn't until she discovered the SuperHabits approach that Sophia began to understand that her challenges were not about discipline, but rather about how her habits were misaligned with her true nature.

In the SuperHabits approach, Sophia learned about the Ayurvedic mind-body types. After taking the quiz, she discovered that she was predominantly Vata, which meant that her mind and body were governed by the elements of air and space. Vata types are known for their lively, creative energy and love of novelty. They are quick to learn but can be easily distracted and tend to struggle with consistency. This made Sophia's previous struggles clear: she was not inherently undisciplined; she was simply trying to adopt habits that didn't fit her natural tendencies.

Understanding this was a breakthrough moment for Sophia. Instead of feeling like a failure, she began to see herself with compassion. She realized that Vata types thrive on variety and spontaneity, which is why rigid routines didn't work for her. The SuperHabits approach offered a personalized approach that allowed Sophia to incorporate changes in a way that was engaging and aligned with her nature.

For example, Sophia introduced small but varied changes to her daily routine. Instead of committing to a single form of exercise, she embraced a mix—yoga on some days, dancing on others, and brisk walks when she felt like getting fresh air. This flexible approach kept her interested and engaged, preventing the boredom that often derailed her previous attempts.

The Ayurvedic Framework: Understanding Your Type

Sophia's story highlights why it is crucial to identify your Ayurvedic mind-body type when adopting new habits. According to Ayurveda, everyone has a unique combination of Vata, Pitta, and Kapha, which shapes their personality, behavior, and physical characteristics. Understanding these doshas helps us identify the most suitable habit-change strategies.

Vata Mind-Body Type: Creativity and Change

Vata mind-body types often have a thin build, they don't gain weight easily, are quick to learn, enthusiastic, and become cold easily. Vata mind-body types can get very excited at the idea of starting a new habit and are quick at grasping new information. Due to Vata's airy nature, they love change and spontaneity and can get bored easily, so when creating habits, it's important to focus on ways to keep things interesting. Vata is composed of the space and air elements.

Vata types, like Sophia, are drawn to novelty and often thrive in dynamic, fast-paced environments. However, their airy nature can lead to a lack of stability, making it difficult to sustain new routines. Vata types often have irregular sleep patterns, fluctuating energy levels, and variable appetites.

- In balance: Vata types are creative, energetic, and clear-minded, with balanced digestion and good circulation.

- Out of balance: They may experience anxiety, fatigue, forgetfulness, and difficulty falling asleep.

Three Tips for Supporting Vata Habit Change:

- Create a regular routine: While Vata types resist rigid schedules, establishing a general daily rhythm can help ground their airy nature. Simple rituals, like a warm morning drink or a consistent bedtime, provide the stability they need.

- Use cues and reminders: Vata types benefit from visual cues and reminders. Sophia found this particularly helpful—she placed colorful sticky notes around her workspace as gentle reminders to take breaks or drink water.

- Simplify goals: Vata types can easily feel overwhelmed by too many options. Breaking habits into small, manageable steps and focusing on one or two changes at a time is more effective than trying to overhaul everything at once. This is true for all types, but especially important for Vata.

Vata Type Super Tip: Change one habit at a time.

Pitta Mind-Body Type: Drive and Ambition

Pitta mind-body types have a medium build, a balanced weight, a sharp intellect, are goal oriented, and can become hot easily. Pitta is composed of fire and water.

Pitta mind-body types are detail-oriented individuals who love planning, creating and fulfilling new habits. They generally have a lot of motivation and determination. However, they can be too hard on themselves or become perfectionists if out of balance. They will benefit from support to accept that life is not always perfect and to find a healthy balance between fulfilling those new habits and having downtime to relax. Pitta types can be ambitious, goal-oriented, and detail-oriented. They are natural leaders who thrive on challenges, but their intense drive can sometimes lead to burnout, irritability, or impatience.

- In balance: Pittas have strong digestion, a sharp intellect, and a radiant complexion.
- Out of balance: They can experience anger, overheating, and digestive issues.

Four Tips for Supporting Pitta Habit Change:
- Set realistic goals: Pittas often set high expectations for themselves, which can lead to frustration if results aren't

immediate. Focusing on process rather than perfection can help maintain motivation.

- Balance work with play: Incorporating downtime into the schedule is essential for Pittas. Sophia's Pitta colleague, Daniel, benefited from adding relaxation breaks to his daily routine, which helped him manage stress.

- Don't skip meals: Being "hangry" is a real thing! Pitta's fiery nature means that they have a strong appetite. If they skip or delay a meal, the heat in their body can increase and can cause them to feel more agitated or short-tempered. Try to organize new habits without interfering with mealtimes.

- Cool down: Pittas need cooling strategies, both physically and mentally. Incorporating cooling foods, calming practices like meditation, and regular hydration can help maintain balance.

Pitta Type Super Tip: Don't let the inability to get it perfect prevent you from starting.

Kapha Mind-Body Type: Stability and Consistency

Kapha types generally have a larger build, a tendency to gain weight, have a good memory, are calm and stable, and can become cool easily. Kapha is associated with earth and water, making them grounded, steady, and calm.

While they excel at maintaining routines once established, they can be slow to get started and may struggle with inertia.

People with a predominantly Kapha mind-body type tend to have a lovely, stable, and grounded nature, making them very supportive. At first, this stable nature can make it harder for them to get motivated when it comes to creating new habits. Once a Kapha gets moving with proper support and the right tools to increase motivation, however, they are great at sticking with their habits and enjoy following them.

- In balance: Kaphas have good stamina, a stable temperament, and strong immunity.

- Out of balance: They can become lethargic, resistant to change, and prone to weight gain.

Three Tips for Supporting Kapha Habit Change:

- Get moving early: Morning exercise is especially beneficial for Kapha types, as it helps energize them for the day ahead. A Kapha client of Sophia's started incorporating morning walks, which boosted her mood and motivation.

- Start small: Kaphas benefit from breaking changes into small, achievable steps. Sophia's Kapha friend, Maria, began her yoga practice with just five minutes a day and gradually built up.

- Involve a buddy: Kaphas thrive on social support. Having an accountability partner can be a game-changer, as it encourages them to stick to new habits.

Kapha Type Super Tip: Get help from friends.

Sophia's Transformation Through Awareness

As Sophia progressed through the SuperHabits program, her understanding of her Vata nature continued to evolve. She began to embrace her spontaneity while also building stability. Her self-talk shifted from self-doubt to gentle encouragement. Whenever she felt herself slipping into old patterns, she reminded herself that it was part of the process and used the tips suited to her Vata type. By the end of the program, Sophia had not only established new habits but had also developed a deeper sense of self-awareness, compassion, and balance.

Conclusion: The Power of Personalized Awareness in Habit Change

Awareness is the foundation of habit change. It allows us to understand who we are, what drives us, and how we can align our habits with our natural tendencies. The Ayurvedic approach to understanding mind-body types—Vata, Pitta, and Kapha—provides a powerful framework for personalization. As Sophia's story illustrates, understanding and embracing your type can transform the habit-change journey from a struggle into an empowering experience of self-discovery.

Now that you have a better awareness of who you are, let's move to the next chapter, where we explore consciousness-based techniques to unlock deeper layers of the mind and enhance your habit-change journey.

SECTION 2

CONSCIOUSNESS

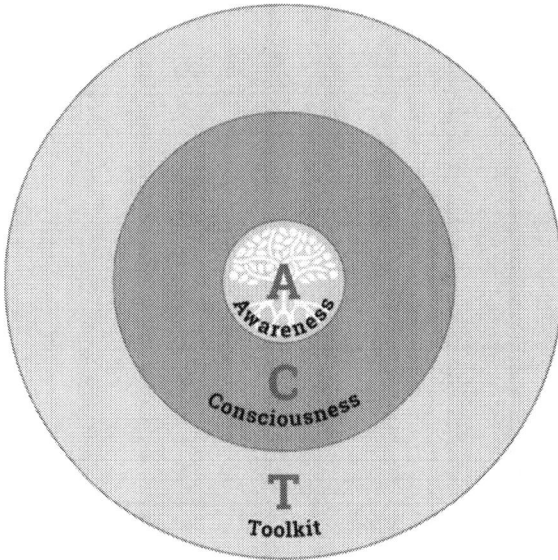

CHAPTER 2

WHAT IS CONSCIOUSNESS?

Until you make the unconscious conscious,
it will direct your life and you will call it fate.

– Carl Jung

Consciousness is one of the most profound and enigmatic subjects in both science and philosophy. It encompasses the essence of awareness, subjective experiences, and the sense of self. The understanding of consciousness varies greatly across different cultures and eras, leading to diverse interpretations and theories. Modern science often considers consciousness an epiphenomenon of the nervous system, while the ancient Vedic perspective regards it as the fundamental source of all existence.

In contemporary science, consciousness is frequently examined through the lens of neuroscience and cognitive science, often viewed as a byproduct of complex neural processes. Modern neuroscience suggests that consciousness arises from neuronal activity in the brain. Neural correlates of consciousness are specific brain states that correspond with particular conscious experiences. For instance, activity in the visual cortex is associated with visual perception, while the prefrontal cortex is linked with higher-order thought processes.

Despite advances in neuroscience, the "hard problem of consciousness," a term coined by philosopher David Chalmers, remains unresolved. This problem refers to the difficulty of explaining why and how physical processes in the brain give rise to subjective experiences. While we can map brain activity and understand the functions of different brain regions, the subjective nature of experience—why seeing the color red feels a certain way—eludes comprehensive explanation.

Maharishi Mahesh Yogi, the founder of the Transcendental Meditation program, collaborated with Nobel laureate physicists to explore the relationship between the unified field of consciousness and the unified field of modern quantum physics. Maharishi introduced Transcendental Meditation as a means of directly experiencing the field of pure consciousness. Dr. Tony Nader, who worked with Maharishi for many years, expands on Maharishi's work in his book *Consciousness Is All There Is*, providing a new integrative theory of consciousness.

Our consciousness-based approach to habit change is inspired by Dr. Nader's analysis of consciousness. The tools we use in the SuperHabits approach allow us to access deeper levels of the mind and ultimately reach the field of pure consciousness—the source of creativity, energy, and intelligence. This gives us a significant advantage in the habit-change process.

The Ocean of Consciousness

Let's once again compare the mind to an ocean. On the surface, the ocean has waves, representing the conscious mind's active thoughts. As you dive deeper, the ocean becomes calmer, akin to the subconscious mind. At the very bottom of this ocean is pure consciousness, the origin of all thought. Pure consciousness expresses itself through thoughts, much like air bubbles rising from the ocean's depths to the surface.

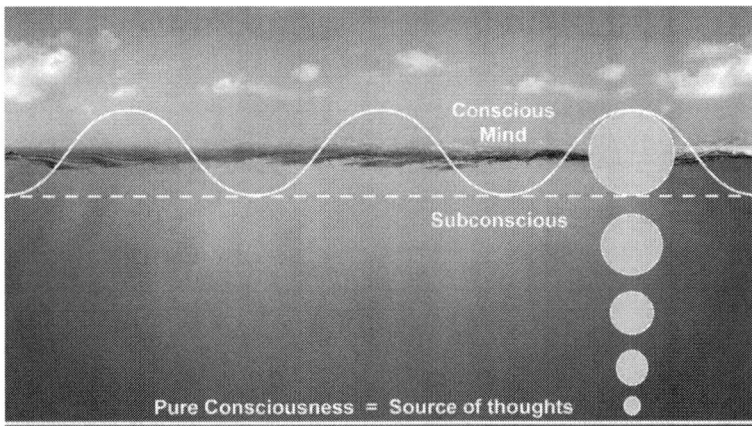

Psychologists discuss the subconscious as an area deep within the mind of which we are not normally aware. Negative experiences stored in the subconscious can lead to self-doubt and self-sabotage, influencing our ability to make changes in our lives. For example, a difficult past relationship might cause anxiety about future relationships, acting like layers of pollution in the ocean of consciousness. These layers can make it harder to adopt new habits, as they block access to the deeper levels of the mind.

But can we remove these deep-rooted stresses that impede habit change? The answer is yes. Consciousness-based tools help dissolve or neutralize these stresses, allowing us to access our pure, true selves and facilitate meaningful habit change.

A Story of Transformation: Michael's journey into consciousness

Michael, a 50-year-old software engineer, had been struggling with stress-related issues for years. He worked long hours at a high-pressure tech company, and while his career was successful, he felt disconnected from himself and those around him. His days were filled with constant mental activity—coding, problem-solving, and managing deadlines. As a result, Michael found it difficult to unwind, and his mind seemed to race even when he tried to relax.

Michael was aware that his stress levels were impacting his health. He often suffered from tension headaches, had trouble sleeping, and felt irritable even during family time. He knew he needed to make changes, but his attempts at adopting new habits, such as regular exercise or an improved diet, failed time and again. He would start enthusiastically, only to be pulled back into old patterns. Michael's problem wasn't motivation; it was a deeper issue of subconscious resistance, compounded by stress.

Feeling frustrated, Michael decided to try a different approach and joined the SuperHabits program, intrigued by its focus on consciousness. Early in the program, Michael was introduced to the concept of the mind as an ocean, with waves representing surface thoughts and the deeper layers representing the subconscious and pure consciousness. The idea that deeper stresses could be blocking his attempts at habit change resonated with him.

He also learned about the importance of transcending sur- face-level thoughts to access the source of creativity and calm within—the field of pure consciousness. Michael was particularly drawn to the practice of Transcendental Meditation (TM), which promised a direct experience of this deeper level. Despite his initial skepticism, he began practicing TM under the guidance of a qualified instructor.

Within weeks of regular practice, Michael started to notice subtle yet significant changes. The first shift was in his mental clarity. The racing thoughts that used to dominate his evenings began to subside, replaced by a sense of inner stillness. He also found that he was less reactive to stressful situations at work; his usual irritation in response to last-minute requests diminished, and he began to approach challenges with a calmer, clearer mind.

Michael's improved mental state had a ripple effect on his efforts to change habits. He found that he no longer needed to force himself to exercise or eat healthier. Instead, these behaviors felt more natural, as his stress-induced resistance had decreased. The mental clarity and calmness he experienced during meditation carried over into his daily life, making habit change easier and more sustainable.

The most profound change, however, was in Michael's sense of identity. Through regular meditation, he began to experience a deeper sense of self, one that wasn't defined by external achievements or stress. He described this transformation as discovering "the silent depths of the ocean" within himself. This shift in identity provided a new motivation for habit change. Instead of focusing on superficial goals like "losing weight" or "getting fit," Michael was driven by a deeper desire for inner peace and well-being.

This identity-based approach changed everything for Michael. He no longer saw meditation and exercise as tasks to check off a to-do list; instead, they became meaningful practices that aligned with his deeper self. The internal language of his mind also shifted from "I have to meditate" to "I want to meditate." This deeper motivation drove a positive cycle of habit change, where each success reinforced his sense of self and built momentum for further change.

Consciousness-Based Techniques

The goal of using a consciousness-based approach is not only to make practical improvements in life but also to help us experience our deeper self. Let's explore some of the techniques that facilitate this process.

Meditation

Meditation is one of the oldest consciousness-based approaches for improving mental, emotional, and physical well-being. We recommend Transcendental Meditation (TM) because it is an evidence-based practice that is easy to learn and practice. TM requires a qualified instructor, which you can find easily at www.tm.org. Scientific research demonstrates that TM positively influences life by improving both physical and mental health. Bad habits like smoking, excessive drinking, and drug abuse are reduced, while anxiety and depression decrease. Simultaneously, creativity, learning ability, and intelligence improve. This is because mental states are closely linked with physiological states, and meditation affects both.

By transcending surface thoughts and experiencing deeper levels of the mind, TM brings us to pure consciousness—a field of bliss, intelligence, and creativity. This experience creates a state of restful alertness, rewiring the brain for greater effectiveness over time. Michael's story is a testament to this: as he meditated regularly, he found it easier to adopt new habits, not because he was forcing change but because his mind was clearer, and his motivation was deeper.

Diaphragmatic Breathing

In addition to meditation, another effective consciousness-based technique is diaphragmatic breathing. By focusing on deep, abdominal breathing, we can reduce stress and enhance mental clarity (see Appendix 4 for detailed description). Diaphragmatic breathing helps normalize the body's stress response, as indicated by lower cortisol levels. This practice not only calms the mind but also prepares it for deeper meditation.

Michael also incorporated diaphragmatic breathing into his routine, especially before meetings or presentations at work. This helped him manage anxiety and maintain a sense of calm. The breathing exercises complemented his meditation practice, creating a sense of balance and centeredness throughout the day.

Pranayama

Pranayama is another tool that bridges the connection between mind and body (See Appendix 5 for detailed instruction). One such technique, Pranayama (comfortable breathing), helps regulate energy flow in the body, promoting overall health and longevity. It involves slow, deep and even breathing, which supports a balanced nervous system and mental stability.

Pranayama practices can be easily integrated into a daily routine and are particularly effective when performed before meditation. Michael found that practicing pranayama before his morning meditation sessions enhanced the depth of his meditation. The slow, intentional breathing helped clear his mind and prepare him to transcend thoughts, accessing deeper levels of consciousness.

Dynamics of Group Consciousness

Another approach used in the SuperHabits program is the dynamics of group consciousness, derived from the Vedic understanding of an underlying field of consciousness that connects individuals within a group. This concept is similar to the idea of corporate culture, but it goes deeper, emphasizing the collective consciousness of a group or society.

In the program, individuals have accountability partners and participate in learning circles, creating a supportive environment that aids habit adoption.

For Michael, the group dynamic was an unexpected but powerful element of his transformation. Being part of a learning circle with others who were also exploring deeper levels of consciousness provided a sense of community and mutual support. This collective consciousness reinforced his individual efforts, making habit change easier and more fun.

Why We Use Consciousness-Based Approaches

How do consciousness-based approaches help us adopt a new habit? Imagine trying to move an iceberg in the ocean. The iceberg appears small on the surface, but its true mass lies beneath the water. Pushing only at the surface achieves little. Similarly, habit change is difficult when addressed solely at the conscious level of the mind. Deeper stresses within the subconscious often block progress. By using consciousness-based approaches, we can access deeper levels of the mind and move past these blocks, making habit change more natural and sustainable.

Consciousness-based approaches also shift motivation from external to internal, aligning it with a deeper sense of identity. As Michael discovered, the most powerful motivation comes from the deepest levels of the ocean of consciousness—where the best version of ourselves resides. This identity-based approach shifts the internal language from "I have to" to "I want to," creating a more positive and enduring drive for change.

Ayurveda and Consciousness

Ayurveda not only personalizes habit change but also emphasizes the role of consciousness in improving health and well-being. Modern neuroscience supports this ancient insight by demonstrating the brain's neuroplasticity—its ability to change and form new neural pathways through repetition and habit. By integrating Ayurveda with consciousness-based techniques, we can address both the mind and body at deeper levels, creating a more holistic approach to habit change.

For example, motivation is sharply influenced by our mind-body type. Understanding your dosha not only helps identify the most suitable habits but also reveals how you can maintain motivation:

- Vata: Enjoys variety and thrives on creative, new experiences. To stay motivated, Vata types should introduce elements of fun into their routines and switch up activities when necessary.

- Pitta: Is driven by goals and achievement. Setting clear, measurable targets is key, but Pittas should also focus on enjoying the process, not just the outcome.

- Kapha: Prefers stability and may need a push to get started. External motivation, like a supportive partner or group, can help Kaphas build momentum until they can sustain habits on their own.

Vata mind-body types are generally quick to learn but they may have a hard time sticking to a new habit and can be overwhelmed by too many choices. If this mind-body type goes off their habit change plan, a partner, friend, or coach will often be very effective in guiding them towards calm positivity and helping them create nourishing and supportive routines.

Pitta mind-body types operate at a medium speed, but they often do things with intensity. This mind-body type has a strong sense of purpose and is goal-oriented. They have no trouble adopting new habits or routines as long as they believe that these will help them accomplish their goals. If they think that a new habit is not supporting their objectives and ambitions, they will soon abandon it.

Kapha mind-body types tend to have a slower, steadier inner rhythm. They also often like to think things through thoroughly and methodically before making decisions, so they may need extra time and encouragement to adjust to a new routine. This mind-body type will be better able to execute habit change when they have some support from a partner or friend.

Conclusion: The Transformative Power of Consciousness

Michael's story shows how accessing deeper levels of consciousness can transform the habit-change process. It's not just about adopting new behaviors; it's about discovering a deeper, more aligned version of yourself. As we explore consciousness-based techniques, remember that true transformation begins beneath the surface, where the waves of daily thoughts give way to the silent depths of pure consciousness.

CHAPTER 3

OVERCOMING RESISTANCE AND BECOMING RESILIENT

Success consists of going from failure to failure without loss of enthusiasm.

– Winston Churchill

Helen Keller was a remarkable advocate, author, and lecturer who overcame incredible challenges to become an iconic figure in the disability rights movement. Keller, who lost both her sight and hearing at a young age, faced immense difficulty in her pursuit of education and independence. Yet, she demonstrated incredible resilience, refusing to be defined by her disabilities. With the help of her devoted teacher, Anne Sullivan, Keller learned to communicate through touch and became the first deaf-blind person to earn a bachelor's degree. Her journey was marked by resistance, but she saw each obstacle as an opportunity for growth and self-discovery.

Keller's story reminds us that resilience is not the absence of resistance; rather, it is the strength to continue moving forward despite it. In the same way, we all face resistance in our lives—whether it is internal (self-doubt, procrastination, fear) or external (criticism, setbacks, unexpected challenges). To overcome these barriers and establish lasting change, we need to cultivate resilience, much like Helen Keller did.

The Neural Basis of Resistance to Change

Resistance to change is not just a psychological phenomenon; it is deeply rooted in the brain's wiring. When we encounter change—whether it's adopting a new habit or responding to a new environment—the brain perceives it as a potential threat. This triggers a response from the amygdala, a small, almond-shaped cluster of neurons responsible for processing fear and initiating the stress response.

When stress becomes chronic, the prefrontal cortex—the part of the brain responsible for reasoning, decision-making, and impulse control—loses its effectiveness. As a result, people often experience difficulty controlling impulses, planning for the future, and maintaining motivation. It's as if the brain is stuck in survival mode, focused on immediate safety rather than long-term goals.

The body's stress response is designed to help us react quickly in dangerous situations, such as encountering a snake. In such cases, the amygdala bypasses the slower-thinking prefrontal cortex to activate the "fight or flight" response. However, when this same stress response is triggered by non-threatening situations, like a challenging work project or a minor disagreement, it can create chronic anxiety. This ongoing state of hyperarousal leads to elevated levels of cortisol, which can damage the hippocampus, an area crucial for memory and emotional regulation.

If we frequently operate in this fight-or-flight mode, the neural circuits for stress become stronger, while the circuits for growth, calm, and creativity weaken. This makes it harder to form and sustain positive habits, even when stress is no longer present. For some, chronic stress can result in a brain that's perpetually stuck in a heightened state of alertness, contributing to conditions like Post-Traumatic Stress Disorder (PTSD) or more common patterns of restlessness and tension.

Imagine stress as rocks that fill a backpack. Each rock represents a past or present stressor. The more rocks you carry, the harder it becomes to move forward, let alone establish new habits. Reducing stress is akin to removing rocks, lightening the load, and improving resilience. While sleep can help, it often only removes the smaller rocks. To address deeper stressors, we need more powerful techniques, like meditation, which access quieter levels of the mind.

Emma's Journey: Building resilience by overcoming resistance

Emma, a 38-year-old elementary school teacher, had always been passionate about her work. She enjoyed helping her students grow, but the demands of teaching, combined with her tendency to take on too many responsibilities, left her feeling perpetually exhausted. Emma wanted to establish healthier habits—like regular exercise, better sleep, and mindful eating—but she struggled with consistency.

Each time Emma attempted to change her habits, she faced resistance. She would start with enthusiasm, only to lose motivation after a week or two. This cycle of excitement followed by burnout left Emma feeling defeated, reinforcing a sense of failure. It was not just physical exhaustion that held her back but also a deep-seated belief that she wasn't capable of lasting change.

Feeling stuck, Emma joined the SuperHabits program in hopes of finding a new approach. Early in the program, she was introduced to the metaphor of the "backpack filled with rocks," which represented the accumulated stresses she carried. This analogy resonated deeply with Emma, as it illustrated why even small changes felt so difficult. Her resistance wasn't simply about willpower; it was the weight of unresolved stress holding her back.

Discovering OPAL: A New Way to Manage Emotions

The program introduced Emma to O.P.A.L., a four-step approach to managing emotions and experiences:

- **O**: Observe: Emma learned to observe her thoughts and emotions without judgment. This step helped her become aware of negative self-talk and stress triggers.

- **P**: Process: She took time to process the reasons behind her thoughts and feelings, identifying patterns that contributed to resistance.

- **A**: Absorb: Emma absorbed the insights gained from processing her emotions, allowing them to inform her decisions and behavior.

- **L**: Let go: Finally, Emma practiced letting go of negative emotions or thoughts that weighed her down, releasing their hold and fostering a sense of freedom.

	Physical Level	Mental/Emotional Level
Observe	Food	Thoughts & Feelings About the Situation
Process	Chew	Identify Your Patterns; Build Self-Awareness
Absorb	Nutrients	Learning & Insights to Help You Grow
Let Go	Of what's not needed	

At first, Emma struggled with observing her emotions without judgment, as she was accustomed to harsh self-criticism. But as she practiced O.P.A.L. regularly, she began to develop greater self-awareness and compassion. She noticed that many of her negative emotions were rooted in unrealistic expectations and perfectionism, which fueled her resistance to change.

35

Reframing: Metabolizing Habit Change

In Ayurveda, the mind and body are viewed as a unified system. What affects one inevitably affects the other. Emma realized that her inability to establish new habits was not just a mental issue but also a physical one, as chronic stress had accumulated in her body over time. Ayurveda emphasizes that focusing on positive thoughts and behaviors strengthens those aspects of the self.

During one of the SuperHabits program's group sessions, Emma encountered an old Cherokee story about a grandfather explaining to his grandson:

"There is a fight between two wolves inside us. One wolf is full of anger, envy, regret, greed, arrogance, and self-pity. The other wolf is full of joy, peace, love, hope, humility, kindness, and compassion."

The grandson asked, "Grandfather, which wolf will win?"

The old Cherokee replied, "The one you feed."

This story resonated with Emma on a profound level. She recognized that by focusing on negative self-talk, she was inadvertently feeding the wrong wolf. Emma committed to shifting her focus to gratitude, self-compassion, and personal growth. She started a gratitude journal, writing down three things she was grateful for each day. This simple practice helped her redirect her energy toward positive emotions, reducing her resistance to new habits.

Strategies to Neutralize Toxic Emotions

Emma also learned how to neutralize toxic emotions, such as blame, defensiveness, stonewalling, and contempt, which can act as barriers to habit change.

Blame

Blame often manifests as aggression—whether directed at others or oneself. Emma had a tendency to blame herself harshly when she failed to meet her expectations. The program taught her to adopt a softer approach, starting with curiosity rather than criticism. For example, instead of saying, "I failed again," she learned to ask, "What can I do differently next time?"

From an Ayurvedic perspective, blame is linked to an imbalanced Pitta Mind-Body State, which is associated with heat, irritability, and impatience. Emma started incorporating cooling foods into her diet, practicing cooling breathing exercises, and taking short breaks throughout the day to maintain her energy balance.

Defensiveness

Defensiveness is a common reaction to criticism, often driven by a fear of failure or rejection. Emma discovered that her defensiveness was rooted in past experiences where she felt judged or misunderstood. To overcome this, she practiced the 2% Rule—considering that at least 2% of what others said might be true. This simple shift allowed her to stay open and curious rather than defensive.

Defensiveness is often associated with an imbalanced Vata Mind-Body State, characterized by anxiety and restlessness. Emma learned to balance this energy through grounding practices, such as warm baths, daily walks, and regular sleep schedules.

Stonewalling

Stonewalling, or withdrawing from situations, was another challenge for Emma. When she felt overwhelmed, she tended to shut down emotionally and avoid difficult conversations. Through the SuperHabits program, she learned to recognize this behavior as a sign of accumulated stress. Emma added regular exercise, such as brisk walks or short runs, to her daily routine. This helped her release tension and approach situations with more openness and engagement.

From an Ayurvedic perspective, stonewalling is linked to an imbalanced Kapha Mind-Body State, which tends toward inertia and withdrawal. To counter this, Emma practiced morning stretches and engaged in energizing activities to stimulate her energy levels.

Contempt

Contempt, which often manifests as sarcasm or disdain, is the most damaging of toxic emotions. While Emma did not struggle with outward expressions of contempt, she realized that she harbored feelings of frustration toward herself when she failed to meet her goals. The program encouraged her to focus on personal development, self-awareness, and self-compassion.

Contempt is primarily linked to an imbalanced Pitta Mind- Body State, as it often stems from unprocessed anger and frustration. Emma learned to manage her Pitta energy by prioritizing rest, hydration, and a balanced routine, which helped reduce feelings of frustration and enhance her emotional resilience.

The Impact of Self-Talk

Emma's journey also highlights the impact of self-talk on resistance and resilience. Negative self-talk was a significant barrier for her, reinforcing feelings of inadequacy. Through the program, Emma learned to reframe her inner dialogue, shifting from criticism to encouragement. For instance:

Instead of "I can't do this," she began saying, "I am learning and improving each day."

Instead of "I'm a failure," she adopted the phrase, "Mistakes are part of growth."

Emma developed a list of positive affirmations, which she repeated each morning. This practice helped her start the day with a more positive mindset, making it easier to embrace new habits.

Three Steps to Freedom:
Emma's strategy for managing cravings

Emma also adopted a three-step strategy to manage cravings and impulses that conflicted with her goals:

1. Delay acting: When faced with a craving, Emma paused and acknowledged it without immediate action. For example, instead of reaching for chocolate after a stressful day, she said to herself, "I see you, craving, but I don't need to act right now."

2. Calm down and create a gap: Emma used breathing techniques, such as diaphragmatic breathing (see Appendix 4) or Sukh-Pranayama (see Appendix 5), to calm her nervous system. This created a mental gap, allowing her to access her rational thinking.

3. Reflect on underlying feelings: Emma then explored the emotions driving her cravings, asking herself, "What am I truly feeling?" Often, she discovered that her cravings were rooted in loneliness, boredom, or fatigue. By identifying these feelings, she was able to redirect her energy toward healthier actions, such as calling a friend or taking a warm bath.

Conclusion: Building Resilience Through Consciousness-Based Tools

Emma's story demonstrates that overcoming resistance is not about pushing harder but about lightening the load in the "backpack" and transforming the inner dialogue. By using consciousness-based tools like meditation, breathing exercises, and OPAL, Emma not only established new habits but also cultivated deeper resilience. Her journey shows that with patience, compassion, and the right strategies, we can all move from resistance to resilience. In the next chapter, we'll explore the specific tools in the SuperHabits Toolkit that can help solidify these changes and enhance your resilience in the face of challenges

CHAPTER 4

MOTIVATION

Men's natures are alike; it is their habits that separate them.

– Confucius

We all share fundamental needs like sustenance, shelter, and security, alongside deeper desires for connection, love, and self-fulfillment. It's this blend of motivations that propels us forward, shaping our journey toward becoming the best version of ourselves. What fuels your quest for knowledge? Is it fear, or is it that spark of inspiration? While fear can be a potent, albeit unpleasant, driver—motivating some through the fear of failure—for many, inspiration ignites the fire within, fueling mental vitality and creative exploration. Having a crystal-clear intent or vision of your destination and goals can be a game-changer. The sharper your focus, the easier it becomes to sort through your desires and channel your energy efficiently.

A Personal Story:
Linda's journey to discovering her motivation

Linda, a 32-year-old software developer, found herself struggling with motivation. Her job was stable, and she was good at it, but she felt stagnant, lacking the drive to pursue her passion for painting. Whenever she tried to set aside time for her creative pursuits, the demands of her daily routine seemed to take precedence. Linda often asked herself, "Why can't I find the motivation to paint regularly when I love it so much?" She felt a growing frustration at the gap between what she truly wanted and what she was actually doing.

When Linda joined the SuperHabits program, she was introduced to the concept of intrinsic and extrinsic motivation. She realized that while painting was intrinsically rewarding, her job and daily responsibilities were governed by extrinsic motivators like paychecks, deadlines, and recognition. By understanding this difference, she learned how to better structure her time and energy. Linda started by setting a simple, clear goal: to paint for 30 minutes, three times a week.

She also created a motivating environment—her small studio was decorated with her favorite colors and art supplies were organized and easily accessible. To maintain consistency, Linda added an extrinsic motivator: she decided to showcase her work on social media every month, adding a layer of external accountability. Gradually, she began to see painting not as something to squeeze in but as a source of joy and personal fulfillment.

Linda's journey from feeling stagnant to reigniting her passion was fueled by the right blend of intrinsic and extrinsic motivators.

The Science of Motivation

Motivation springs from both internal (intrinsic) and external (extrinsic) sources of gratification. Internally, the sense of joy, fulfillment, and achievement derived from an activity drives us forward. Externally, rewards like recognition, praise, money, or perks act as fuel to propel us further. For example, in Linda's case, the joy of painting was an intrinsic motivator, while showcasing her work publicly provided an extrinsic boost.

Intrinsic Motivation: The Inner Drive

Intrinsic motivation is tied to the basic psychological needs of autonomy, competence, and relatedness. It involves engaging in activities for the pure pleasure and satisfaction they bring, such as pursuing a hobby, reading a book, or learning a new skill. Activities driven by intrinsic motivation are more likely to be sustained over time because they fulfill these core needs.

For example, Linda's passion for painting was intrinsically motivated because it allowed her to express herself freely (autonomy), improve her skills (competence), and connect with her creativity (relatedness).

Extrinsic Motivation: The External Push

Extrinsic motivation, on the other hand, involves engaging in behaviors for rewards that are separate from the activity itself, like recognition, money, or avoiding criticism. In Linda's case, the decision to share her paintings on social media provided a form of external accountability, making her more committed to her painting schedule.

However, extrinsic motivators have limitations. They can be effective for starting a new behavior but may not sustain it in the long run. Research on the overjustification effect has shown that when people receive extrinsic rewards for activities they already enjoy, their intrinsic motivation can diminish. Balancing both forms of motivation is essential for creating lasting habit change.

Neuroscience of Motivation

Motivation is deeply rooted in the brain's structure and chemistry. By understanding the neurological basis of motivation and incorporating consciousness-based strategies, we can harness this powerful force to achieve our goals and transform our habits.

Key Brain Regions in Motivation

- The prefrontal cortex: Associated with planning, decision-making, and self-control, it helps us set goals, make plans, and resist temptations that might derail progress.

- The nucleus accumbens: Often referred to as the brain's "reward center," it activates during pleasurable experiences or the anticipation of rewards, playing a crucial role in releasing dopamine.

- The amygdala: Involved in processing emotions like fear and pleasure, it influences our motivation by shaping responses to potential rewards and threats.

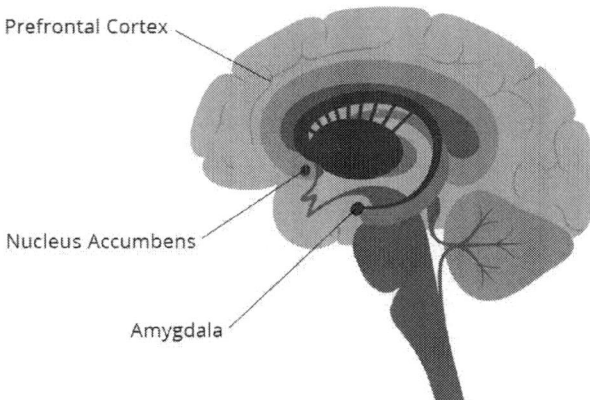

Prefrontal Cortex

Nucleus Accumbens

Amygdala

The Role of Dopamine in Motivation

Dopamine, a neurotransmitter, is central to the brain's reward system. It regulates various functions, including motivation, movement, and emotional responses. Here's how dopamine contributes to our motivation:

Anticipation of Rewards

Dopamine is activated when we anticipate activities that fulfill basic needs or bring pleasure, such as eating, socializing, or achieving goals. For example, when Linda anticipated the pleasure of painting, dopamine was released, reinforcing her motivation to start painting more frequently.

Cues in the Environment

Cues in our environment can activate the dopamine system, creating a craving for the anticipated reward. For instance, the sight of Linda's organized art supplies served as a visual cue, triggering her desire to paint.

Habit Formation

Dopamine plays a pivotal role in forming habits. The more a behavior is reinforced by dopamine release, the stronger and more automatic it becomes. This process explains why habits—both good and bad—can be difficult to break.

The Power of Goals

Goals act as powerful motivators because they provide clear direction and purpose. They tap into the dopamine reward system, creating anticipation and excitement about achieving desired outcomes. Linda's goal of painting three times a week helped her maintain focus, while the dopamine release from small victories (like completing a painting) kept her motivated.

Breaking Goals into Manageable Tasks

Large goals can be overwhelming, but breaking them into smaller tasks makes them more manageable and motivating. For Linda, committing to just 30 minutes of painting allowed her to build consistency without feeling overwhelmed. Each completed session triggered a dopamine release, creating a positive feedback loop that reinforced her painting habit.

Motivation and Your Mind-Body Type

The SuperHabits approach incorporates Ayurveda to personalize motivation strategies based on individual mind-body types. Understanding your type can help tailor your approach to habit change:

In Linda's case, she displayed traits of Vata—enthusiastic about painting but easily distracted by daily responsibilities. To sustain motivation, she combined intrinsic joy with the external accountability of social media sharing, achieving a balanced approach.

Boosting Intrinsic Motivation through Consciousness-Based Approaches

The SuperHabits approach uses techniques to increase intrinsic motivation across all energy types. By diving into consciousness-based practices like Transcendental Meditation, you can tap into deeper levels of creative intelligence, which enhances clarity and motivation for habit change.

Redefining Motivation for Success

To fully understand your own motivation, consider these strategies:

- Identify your core values: Understanding what matters most to you can help align goals with intrinsic motivation. For Linda, painting was aligned with her value of creative expression.

- Leverage intrinsic rewards: Focus on the inner satisfaction of achieving goals rather than external rewards. Linda found that the joy of painting was a strong intrinsic motivator, which sustained her long-term commitment.

- Celebrate small wins: Reinforce motivation by celebrating each step toward your goal, no matter how small. Every painting Linda completed provided a burst of dopamine, reinforcing her commitment to the habit.

Conclusion: Ignite Your Inner Motivation

Linda's journey shows that with the right blend of intrinsic and extrinsic motivation, you can reignite your passion, achieve your goals, and transform your habits. By understanding the neuroscience of motivation, setting clear goals, and personalizing strategies based on your mind-body type, you can sustain lasting change.

Motivation is not just about external rewards; it's about aligning your actions with your core values, embracing the joy of progress, and tapping into deeper sources of creative intelligence. Keep experimenting, keep celebrating, and let the fire of motivation guide you toward a more fulfilling life.

SECTION 3
TOOLKIT

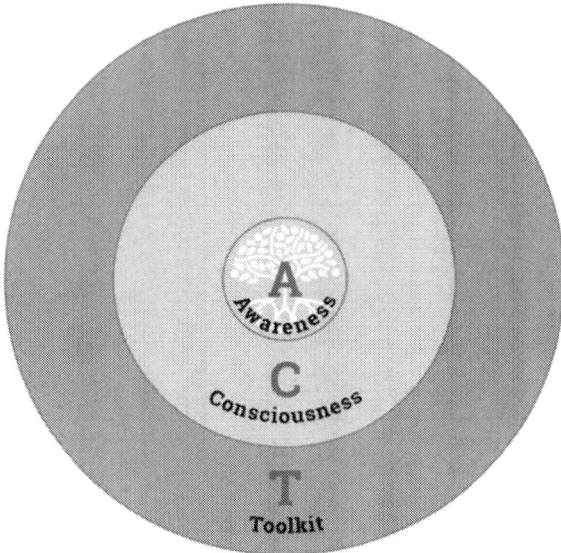

CHAPTER 5

TOOLKIT

Character is simply habit long continued.

– Plutarch

One of the main tools in the SuperHabits approach is the Habit Map, a practical, visual aid designed to help create and maintain habits. It serves as a step-by-step guide to break down goals into actionable steps, making it easier to stay consistent and track progress. The Habit Map is adaptable to any type of habit change, making it a versatile tool that supports your personal growth journey.

How to Create a Habit Map

To create your Habit Map, start with a blank piece of paper or a digital document. In the center, write your main intention or desire for habit change. Around this central hub, draw spokes like a wheel, each representing an action step toward achieving your goal. Next, prioritize these steps, focusing on the most important one. Consider what cues or prompts will remind you to engage in the new habit. Finally, decide how to measure your progress and set a reward for establishing your new habit or eliminating your old one. You can see these steps visually on the Habit Map picture:

1. Start with a clear intention: For example, write, "I want to lose 15 pounds over three months" at the center of your Habit Map.

2. Explore action steps: Identify three ways to achieve this goal, such as exercising more, eating a lighter dinner, or making lunch your main meal.

3. Prioritize steps: Number your action steps in order of importance or ease of implementation.

4. Add a cue: Choose a cue or prompt to remind you to engage in the habit, like a phone reminder or a sticky note on the fridge.

5. Measure success: Track your progress, such as weighing yourself daily or recording meal choices in a journal.

6. Choose a reward: Decide on a reward for your progress, like treating yourself to a book, a new fitness accessory, or enjoying a weekend activity.

Experiment and adjust: If you aren't getting the desired results, revise your action steps and try again.

SuperHabits Map

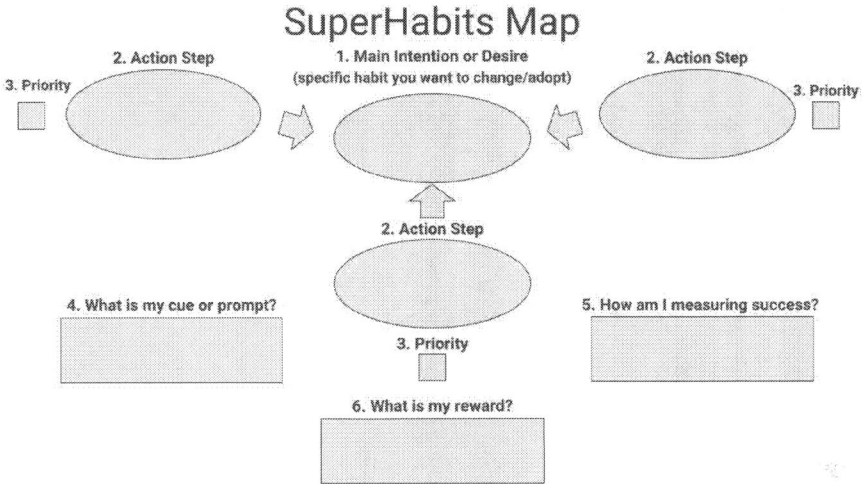

The Habit Map is just one of many tools in the SuperHabits Toolkit, which also includes four coaching techniques: Self-Coaching, Partner Coaching, Group Coaching, and Environmental Coaching.

A Personal Story: David's journey with the Toolkit

David, a 45-year-old marketing executive, had struggled with poor eating habits, inconsistent exercise, and a general feeling of being "stuck" for years. Despite his desire to adopt a healthier lifestyle, the demands of his job and frequent travel made it difficult to stay consistent with any wellness plan. David would often start strong with a new diet or workout routine, only to abandon it weeks later due to stress or a busy schedule.

When David joined the SuperHabits program, he was initially unsure if the simple tools would be effective. But as he started working with the Habit Map, he saw how it offered a clear, visual guide to his goals. At the center of his Habit Map, David wrote: Lose 10 pounds in three months. Around this core goal, he outlined three action steps: (1) walk for 30 minutes daily, (2) replace sugary snacks with healthier options, and (3) eat a lighter dinner. He prioritized the daily walk as the first step since he felt it would be easiest to implement.

David set a cue by placing his walking shoes by the front door each night and set a phone reminder to take a break and walk. He tracked his daily steps with a fitness app, setting an initial goal of 7,000 steps per day. His reward was a simple treat: if he met his weekly walking goal, he allowed himself a relaxed evening with a favorite movie.

Expanding the Use of the Habit Map

The Habit Map can be customized for various goals beyond weight loss or fitness. Here's how it can be adapted for reducing stress:

1. Clear intention: Reduce daily stress and increase relaxation.

2. Action steps: (1) Practice 20 minutes of Transcendental Meditation twice daily, (2) engage in deep breathing exercises during breaks, and (3) take a nature walk once a week.

3. Prioritize: Start with meditation, as it can be done anywhere.

4. Cue: Use an app to remind you to meditate each morning.

5. Measure success: Track the number of meditation sessions completed weekly.

6. Reward: Treat yourself to a relaxing bath or a favorite book at the end of a successful week.

SuperHabits Map

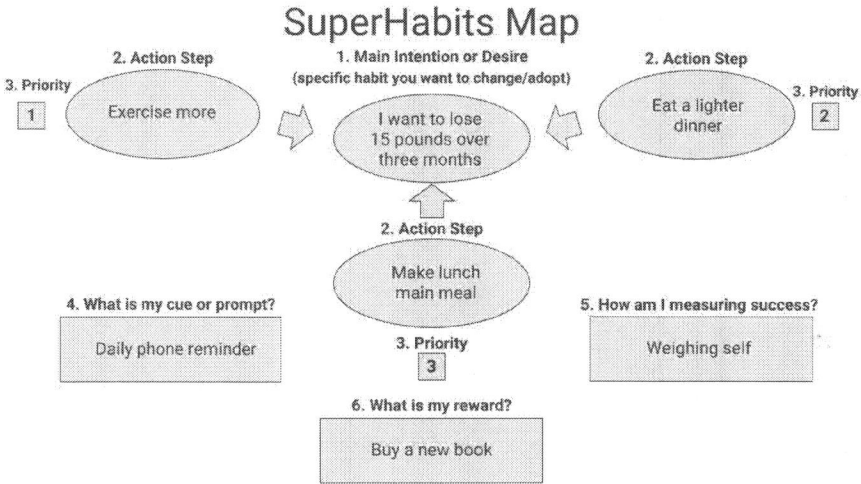

This flexibility makes the Habit Map a versatile tool that supports a wide range of habit changes, from productivity to personal growth.

The Four Coaching Techniques in the Toolkit

The SuperHabits Toolkit incorporates four main coaching techniques, each offering unique benefits and designed to maximize results:

Self-Coaching: Reflecting, Tracking, and Adapting

Self-coaching is an essential tool for personal growth, involving regular reflection, tracking progress, and adapting strategies.

- Journaling: David found that writing in his journal each morning clarified his thoughts and identified triggers for unhealthy eating, such as stress after meetings or boredom in the evenings.

- Tracking sheets: A simple tracking sheet on his refrigerator helped David visually monitor his walking and eating habits, keeping him accountable and motivated.

- Daily reflection: David spent five minutes each evening reflecting on what went well and what needed adjustment, allowing him to tweak his approach as needed.

Practices, such as meditation or breathing exercises, are also key components of self-coaching. These practices help individuals stay present, manage impulses, and maintain focus on their goals.

Partner Coaching: Accountability and Motivation

The partner system is a critical element of the SuperHabits program, providing motivation, accountability, and support. Studies suggest that having an accountability partner increases the likelihood of habit success by up to 65%.

David's accountability partner, Rachel, checked in twice a week. Rachel's support was invaluable when David faced setbacks. For example, when he struggled with late-night snacking, Rachel suggested replacing snacks with a cup of herbal tea. This small change made a big difference.

Rachel also used the active question approach, inspired by Marshall Goldsmith, to help shift focus from outcomes to effort. Instead of asking, "Did you complete your habit today?" the question becomes, "Did you do your best to work on this habit today?" This reframing emphasizes personal effort and encourages self-reflection, helping individuals remain committed without feeling discouraged by setbacks.

Group Coaching: Learning Circles and Peer Support

Learning circles are small groups that meet regularly to discuss progress, share experiences, and offer mutual support. Social support has been shown to significantly improve habit adherence by creating a sense of community and accountability.

David's learning circle met weekly for a 30-minute virtual session. The group operated under four agreements:

1. Safety & support: Participants felt safe to share openly.

2. Be present: Members actively participated and focused on each other's stories.

3. Stay curious: Group members asked open-ended questions and remained curious.

4. Lean in: Everyone was encouraged to engage fully.

Best Practices for Learning Circles

1. Safety & Support

2. Be Present

3. Stay Curious

4. Lean In

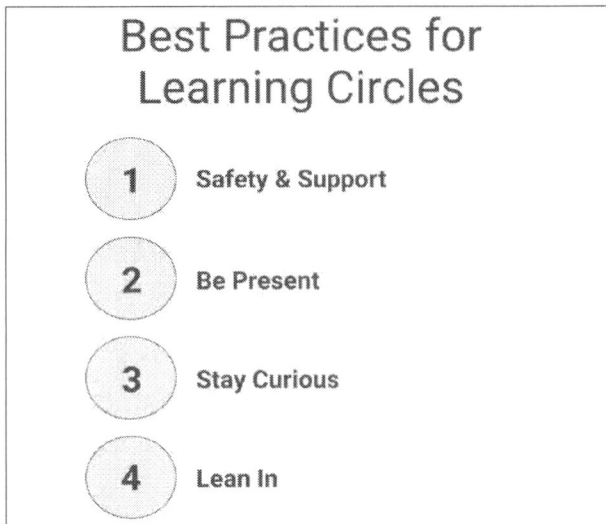

For David, the learning circle provided not only accountability but also new ideas. When David struggled with portion control at dinner, a group member suggested using smaller plates, a simple but effective visual cue.

Environmental Coaching: Optimizing Your Surroundings

Environmental coaching involves creating physical changes to your surroundings to support habit change.

David made several adjustments to his environment:

- Clearing the pantry: He removed junk food from his home, replacing it with healthier snacks like nuts and fruit.

- Visual cues: He placed a large water bottle on his desk to remind himself to stay hydrated and set out his workout clothes the night before.

- Meal prep: He dedicated Sunday afternoons to preparing healthy meals, reducing the temptation to order takeout after a busy day.

Environmental coaching can extend to workspaces, such as organizing a desk to promote focus or creating a calming corner for meditation breaks.

Social Support & Mind-Body Type

Social support is most effective when personalized to an individual's mind-body type:

- Vata types, who thrive on variety but struggle with consistency, benefit from a more grounded partner, like a Kapha, to maintain focus.

- Pitta types, who are goal-oriented but can be intense, benefit from partners who help them relax and enjoy the process.

- Kapha types, who move at a slower pace, benefit from more active partners, like Pittas, to maintain momentum.

David's partnership with Rachel exemplified complementary mind-body types. Rachel's calm Kapha energy balanced David's intense Pitta drive, creating a dynamic that benefited both.

The SMART and SMARTER Frameworks: Setting Effective Goals

The S.M.A.R.T. framework is a widely recognized tool for setting effective goals, ensuring that they are Specific, Measurable, Achievable, Relevant, and Time-bound. In the SuperHabits approach, this framework is further enhanced with the S.M.A.R.T.E.R. acronym, which adds two crucial elements: Ethical and Reevaluate.

S.M.A.R.T.E.R. Goal Setting Explained

- **S**: Specific: A goal should be clear, detailed, and unambiguous. For example, instead of saying, "Get fit," a specific goal would be, "Walk 7,000 steps daily for the next month." Specificity helps define the exact habit you want to adopt, making it easier to focus and take action.

- **M**: Measurable: To effectively track progress, a goal should include measurable elements. In David's case, measuring steps per day provided a clear metric for evaluating progress. Measuring your habit change helps you understand whether you are making progress and allows you to celebrate milestones along the way.

- **A:** Achievable: An achievable goal should stretch your abilities but still be realistic. For David, setting a goal of walking 7,000 steps a day was challenging yet attainable, given his schedule. This principle helps prevent frustration from setting unrealistic goals.

- **R:** Relevant: A relevant goal aligns with your broader objectives and values. David's goal of walking daily aligned with his desire for improved health and weight loss, making it meaningful and motivating.

- **T:** Time-bound: A goal should have a deadline to create a sense of urgency. For instance, David's goal was to lose 10 pounds in three months. Setting a time frame helps maintain focus and encourages consistent action.

- **E:** Ethical: Goals should align with your values and principles. Ethical goals ensure that the methods used to achieve them are fair, just, and socially responsible. For David, this meant choosing healthy, sustainable methods for weight loss, like regular walking and mindful eating, rather than crash diets or unhealthy restrictions. Ethical alignment adds a layer of integrity to the habit-change process, ensuring that it enhances rather than compromises your well-being.

- **R:** Reevaluate: Periodic reassessment of your goals is crucial to ensure they remain relevant, realistic, and aligned with your current circumstances. Re-evaluation allows for adjustments, helping you adapt to changes and refine your approach. For example, David initially set a goal of walking 10,000 steps daily, but he realized it was too ambitious given his work schedule. By reassessing his goal, he adjusted it to 7,000 steps, making it more achievable while maintaining progress.

The S.M.A.R.T.E.R. framework helps individuals set goals that are not only clear and measurable but also aligned with their values and adaptable to changing circumstances. This approach encourages a deeper connection to your goals, enhancing motivation and making habit change more sustainable.

Conclusion: Why the Toolkit Matters

David's story illustrates how the SuperHabits Toolkit can turn intentions into reality. The tools—such as the Habit Map, self-coaching, partner coaching, group coaching, and environmental coaching—gave David the structure and support he needed to make lasting changes. The addition of the S.M.A.R.T.E.R. framework ensured that his goals were not only clear and measurable but also aligned with his values and adaptable to real-life challenges.

The Toolkit is more than just a collection of strategies; it's a personalized approach that adapts to your unique needs, making habit change both rewarding and sustainable. As Mark Twain wisely said, "A habit cannot be tossed out the window; it must be coaxed down the stairs a step at a time."

No matter your mind-body type—Vata, Pitta, or Kapha—the SuperHabits Toolkit provides the tools to create positive, lasting changes, reinforcing the idea that habit change is a journey of small steps and continual adjustments.

CHAPTER 6

MICRO HABITS

Your beliefs become your thoughts.
Your thoughts become your words.
Your words become your actions.
Your actions become your habits.
Your habits become your values.
Your values become your destiny.

– Gandhi

Ever feel like you're stuck in a cycle? You know what you want to change, but making it happen seems impossible. We've all been there. The gap between intentions and reality can feel overwhelming, especially when we aim to make big changes. But what if I told you that small, almost invisible habits, practiced daily, could completely shift your life? These "micro habits" are the secret sauce for real, lasting change. Let's explore how tiny tweaks in your day can help you achieve big wins.

The Power of Micro Habits: Start Small, Dream Big

Micro habits are tiny, easily repeatable actions that require minimal effort but can lead to significant changes over time. Think of them as the building blocks of larger habits. The beauty of micro habits lies in their simplicity—they are so small that they bypass the brain's resistance to change.

A Personal Story: Sarah's journey with micro habits

Sarah, a 38-year-old elementary school teacher, felt constantly overwhelmed by her busy schedule. Juggling lesson planning, parent meetings, and after-school activities left little time for self-care. Despite her efforts to establish healthier routines, Sarah often found herself exhausted by the end of the day, with little energy left to exercise or eat well.

When Sarah joined the SuperHabits program, she was introduced to the concept of micro habits. Instead of trying to make drastic changes, Sarah started with tiny, sustainable shifts. Her first micro habit? Drinking a glass of water before her morning coffee. It seemed almost too simple, but it set a positive tone for the day.

As Sarah continued to build her micro habits, she added a two-minute breathing exercise during her lunch break, a short walk around the block after work, and a consistent bedtime routine. These small, incremental changes not only improved her energy but also helped her establish a sense of control over her day. Over time, Sarah built a solid foundation for larger habits, like a regular 20-minute workout and a balanced meal plan.

When something's off in your body—like a stomachache or poor sleep—it affects your mood, focus, and decision-making. The mind and body are deeply interconnected, and imbalances in one can impact the other. By strengthening the mind-body connection through micro habits, you can make lasting changes more easily.

Micro Habits for Strengthening the Mind-Body Connection

Sarah's first micro habit, drinking a glass of water before her morning coffee, may seem small, but it created a domino effect. Hydrating her body early in the day made her feel more alert and encouraged healthier decisions throughout the morning.

Over time, she added a micro habit of eating a piece of fruit with breakfast, which improved her digestion and boosted her energy levels. The saying, "You are what you eat," emphasizes the strong link between diet and mental clarity. The gut-brain axis is a two-way communication system between the gut and the brain, meaning that an unhealthy gut can lead to brain fog, mood swings, and even anxiety.

Small Dietary Changes with Big Impact

Instead of trying to overhaul your diet all at once, start with small changes:

- Add an extra serving of vegetables: For instance, Sarah began by adding an extra handful of spinach to her morning omelet. This simple change increased her nutrient intake and improved her digestion.

- Swap sugary snacks for nuts: Sarah replaced her usual afternoon chocolate bar with a small handful of almonds. This micro habit not only stabilized her energy but also helped her avoid the post-snack sugar crash.

These micro habits gradually improved Sarah's focus and mood. By making small dietary adjustments, she found it easier to stay energized throughout her busy school days.

Tailoring Your Diet to Your Mind-Body Type

In Ayurveda, understanding your mind-body type (Vata, Pitta, Kapha) can help tailor your dietary habits:

- Vata types: Benefit from warm, nourishing meals. Micro habits like adding a warm soup to lunch or drinking ginger tea in the afternoon can be helpful.

- Pitta types: Need cooling foods to balance their fiery nature. Micro habits like including cucumber slices in meals or sipping coconut water can maintain Pitta balance.

- Kapha types: Need lighter, energizing foods. Micro habits like starting the day with warm lemon water or opting for salads at lunch can help manage weight and energy.

Sarah, whose Kapha energy often made her feel sluggish, found that adding lemon to her water and having a lighter lunch improved her midday energy levels.

Move a Little, Gain a Lot: Micro Habits for Physical Activity

Physical activity doesn't have to mean a full workout. Micro habits like taking a short walk or stretching for a few minutes can significantly boost mental clarity and overall well-being.

Micro Habits for Movement

- Take a 5-minute walk: Sarah began taking a five-minute walk around the schoolyard during her lunch break. This small habit gave her a mental reset and improved her mood.

- Stretch after waking up: Start your day with a two-minute stretch. It wakes up the body and stimulates blood flow, making you feel more alert.

- Stand up every hour: Set a timer to stand up and stretch briefly every hour. This micro habit reduces stiffness and increases productivity.

Sarah's two-minute stretching routine each morning helped her feel more energized. She gradually increased her movement throughout the day, eventually adding a short evening walk to unwind.

Tailoring Exercise to Your Mind-Body Type

Ayurveda emphasizes personalized exercise routines based on mind-body types:

- Vata types: Need moderate activities like yoga, dancing, or gentle walks. Micro habits could include a short, calming walk or five minutes of gentle yoga stretches.

- Pitta types: Thrive on intense workouts but need to cool down afterward. Micro habits for Pittas include ending a workout with a cool shower or taking a dip in a pool.

- Kapha types: Benefit from energizing activities like brisk walking, cycling, or cardio exercises. Micro habits could include a morning jog or jumping jacks to kickstart the day.

Sleep: The Ultimate Reset Button

Sleep is crucial for physical and mental health. It's the body's natural reset button, helping repair tissues, clear toxins, and consolidate memories. Many people struggle with sleep, but micro habits can help establish a more restful routine.

Micro Habits for Better Sleep

- Set a consistent bedtime: Even if it's just 15 minutes earlier than usual, aim to go to bed at the same time each night.

- Limit screen time: Turn off screens 30 minutes before bed to reduce blue light exposure and improve melatonin production.

- Create a relaxing pre-bedtime routine: Light a candle, play soft music, or read a calming book before bed.

Sarah, a natural night owl, struggled to establish a regular sleep schedule. By starting with a micro habit of turning off her phone by 9:30 p.m., she found it easier to wind down and fall asleep.

Tailoring Sleep to Your Mind-Body Type

- Vata types: May struggle with falling asleep. Micro habits like sipping warm milk or listening to soothing music before bed can help.

- Pitta types: Often wake up during the night. Micro habits like drinking cooling herbal tea before bed and keeping the bedroom cool can help.

- Kapha types: Fall asleep easily but struggle to wake up. Micro habits like placing an alarm clock across the room or taking a brisk walk in the morning can help.

Morning Sunlight: A Natural Energy Boost

Morning sunlight helps to regulate your body's internal clock, ensuring that hormones like cortisol and melatonin are properly balanced.

Micro Habits for Getting Morning Sunlight

- Step outside for 5 minutes: Start your day by stepping outside, even if it's just on a balcony or porch. It is best to not wear sunglasses for at least part of the time, but don't strain your eyes by looking directly into the sun.

- Eat breakfast by a window: If stepping outside isn't possible, have your breakfast near an open window to let the sun rays reach the retina in your eyes and warm your skin without glass in the way.

- Use a full-spectrum lamp: If you live in an area with limited sunlight, consider using a full-spectrum lamp.

Sarah created a micro habit of standing on her porch for five minutes each morning with her coffee. This simple shift helped regulate her sleep-wake cycle and improved her overall mood.

Meditation: Your Daily Stress Detox

Meditation is a powerful tool for reducing stress and enhancing mental clarity. Even a few minutes of focused breathing can make a significant difference.

Micro Habits for Meditation

- If meditation feels daunting, begin with just two minutes of diaphragmatic breathing or pranayama.

- Incorporate meditation into your daily routine: Meditate twice a day in the morning and evening.

- We recommend learning Transcendental Meditation since it is easy and well researched.

Sarah felt overwhelmed by the idea of meditation but began with a two-minute breathing exercise during lunch breaks. This micro habit helped her feel more centered, eventually increasing to 10-minute sessions in the mornings.

It is all about making small, incremental tweaks and sticking with them. Micro habits work because they are simple enough to be done consistently, building momentum that can lead to lasting transformation.

By focusing on consistency rather than intensity, you create a foundation of small wins that boost motivation and reinforce positive behavior over time. Each micro habit—whether it's drinking an extra glass of water, getting five minutes of morning sunlight, or meditating for two minutes—adds up gradually, creating a foundation for bigger transformations.

Key Principles for Building Micro Habits

- Make it easy: Choose habits so small they almost seem too simple to fail. For example, Sarah started with a micro habit of drinking one extra glass of water each morning, which set the tone for a healthier day.

- Be consistent: Aim for daily practice, even if it's just a minute or two. Consistency is more impactful than doing something big once in a while. Sarah's two-minute breathing exercises may have seemed minimal, but they became a staple of her routine and paved the way for longer meditation sessions.

- Stack your habits: Attach a new micro habit to an existing habit to create a natural flow. For example, drink water immediately after brushing your teeth, or take a short walk after lunch. Habit stacking ensures that the new behavior has a reliable trigger.

- Celebrate wins: Reinforce success by celebrating even small achievements. Sarah celebrated each week she maintained her micro habits by treating herself to a new book or a relaxing bath, reinforcing her sense of accomplishment.

- Track progress: Keep a simple record of your micro habits. A checkmark on a calendar, a note in a journal, or an entry in a habit-tracking app can provide visual confirmation of your progress and increase motivation.

Micro Habits Across Different Areas of Life

Micro habits can extend beyond physical health to improve mental well-being, productivity, relationships, and personal growth. Here's how they can be applied in different areas:

Micro Habits for Mental Well-Being

- Gratitude practice: Write down one thing you're grateful for each morning. This simple habit shifts your focus toward positivity and can improve overall mental health.

- Deep breathing: Take a 30-second break during the day to focus on your breath. This brief pause reduces stress and improves focus.

Micro Habits for Productivity

Prioritize tasks: At the start of each workday, write down the three most important tasks to complete. This small step can significantly improve focus and productivity.

Declutter for 5 minutes: Spend just five minutes tidying your workspace at the end of the day. This makes it easier to start the next day fresh and focused.

Micro Habits for Relationships

- Daily compliments: Make it a habit to offer one genuine compliment each day to a family member, friend, or colleague.

- Express gratitude: At the end of the day, reflect and consider sharing one positive interaction you had with someone.

Micro Habits for Personal Growth

- Read for 5 minutes: Commit to reading for just five minutes each day. Over time, this can help build a consistent reading habit.

- Reflect in a journal: Write down one lesson you learned or one insight gained at the end of each day.

Conclusion: Transform Your Life One Micro Habit at a Time

Sarah's journey illustrates how small, consistent actions can have a big impact. By focusing on tiny, manageable shifts, she not only improved her physical health but also created mental resilience and emotional balance. Micro habits may seem insignificant at first glance, but their power lies in their simplicity and consistency.

Micro habits serve as stepping stones for bigger transformations. By starting small and maintaining consistency, you can overcome the inertia of old habits and gradually build a healthier, happier, and more balanced life. Remember, the key to lasting change is not intensity but consistency.

As you continue on your journey, remember that micro habits are the foundation of sustainable growth. Each small step is a victory, reinforcing your commitment to a better version of yourself. As the old saying goes, "Little by little, a little becomes a lot."

Start with one micro habit today and watch how it sets the stage for more significant, long-lasting transformation in your life.

CHAPTER 7

ADOPTING A GROWTH MINDSET

Failure is the price of achievement on the success journey.

– John C. Maxwell

We've talked about how our language can influence our actions. A simple shift in words, like moving from "I should" to "I choose to," empowers us and boosts our energy. But the ultimate transformation comes from adopting a growth mindset, which allows us to see every experience— no matter how challenging—as an opportunity for learning and growth. A growth mindset fosters curiosity, enthusiasm, and resilience, making it easier to learn new habits and embrace change.

A fixed mindset, on the other hand, tends to keep people stuck. It limits potential and prevents personal growth, often leading to plateaus in performance and achievement. People with a growth mindset not only achieve more but also maintain confidence, even when progress is slow. This confidence is vital when trying to adopt new habits or learn new skills.

A Personal Story:
Andrew's journey from fixed to growth mindset

Andrew, a 45-year-old graphic designer, had always struggled with perfectionism. He often approached new projects with the thought, "If I can't do it perfectly, I shouldn't do it at all." This fixed mindset kept him from taking risks, trying new design techniques, or exploring creative ideas. When it came to personal habits, the same mindset held him back. Andrew wanted to start a morning exercise routine, but every time he missed a day, he would label himself as a failure and give up entirely.

When Andrew joined the SuperHabits program, he learned about the growth mindset and how it could transform his approach to habit change. Instead of focusing on immediate results, he began to see each attempt as a learning opportunity. He replaced self-criticism with self-compassion, reminding himself that every setback was a stepping stone rather than a stumbling block. Andrew's first breakthrough came when he missed three consecutive days of his exercise routine. Instead of giving up, he applied a growth mindset strategy: he analyzed what led to the missed days, adjusted his schedule, and resumed the habit without guilt. Over time, Andrew became more comfortable with trying new things, both in his design work and his personal life.

Strategies for Shifting to a Growth Mindset

Adopting a growth mindset involves cultivating certain attitudes and strategies. Here are five effective ways to shift toward a growth mindset:

Strategy 1: Shift into Learning

See challenges as learning opportunities rather than setbacks. Instead of asking, "Why is this happening to me?" ask, "What can I learn from this?" This small change in perspective reframes the experience from one of loss to one of growth. Andrew, for instance, began asking himself, "What can I learn from this design not turning out as planned?" This shifted his focus from failure to exploration.

Strategy 2: Mind the Gap

The space between stimulus and response is where you have the power to choose your reaction. For example, if it starts raining on a day you planned to play golf, you can either feel frustrated or embrace it as an opportunity to read a book or try a new indoor activity. The same stimulus can produce different results depending on the mindset. Andrew applied this concept when a client rejected one of his designs—he chose to see it as an opportunity to refine his skills.

Strategy 3: Choose Now

This strategy involves fully accepting the present moment and making the best of it. If an unexpected event disrupts your plans, ask yourself, "Given what's happening, how can I make the best of this?" Instead of wishing things were different, focus on what can be done now. For Andrew, this meant focusing on small, achievable goals in his exercise routine when unexpected work deadlines arose.

Strategy 4: Stop Awful-izing

Awful-izing is when you fixate on the worst possible outcome, creating unnecessary stress. To counter this tendency, become aware of other possibilities. When you notice yourself dwelling on a negative outcome, consciously consider alternative, more positive scenarios. For Andrew, this meant reframing a failed design pitch from, "My career is over," to, "This is a chance to get feedback and improve my work."

Strategy 5: Wear New Shoes

Sometimes, we are too close to a situation to see it objectively. Imagine stepping into someone else's shoes and viewing the situation from their perspective. This can provide valuable insights and new solutions. Andrew found that when he imagined how a successful designer he admired would handle a setback, he felt more open to experimentation and growth.

Falling Forward: Embracing Failure as Part of Success

Failure isn't the opposite of success; it's a critical part of the journey. The key is to fail intelligently—slowing down long enough to reflect on the experience, identify what went wrong, and then adapt your strategy. The cycle of success can be seen as a continuous loop: test, fail, learn, improve, reenter.

Success Cycles

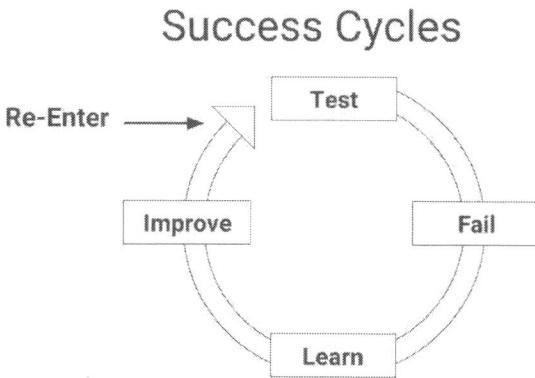

Andrew experienced this cycle firsthand when launching a new design project that flopped. Instead of giving up, he analyzed what went wrong—timing, target audience, and messaging. With this new understanding, he adapted his approach, applied the lessons learned, and tried again. This perspective not only led to a successful project but also increased his confidence to take on new challenges.

Redefining Failure and Success

Many people define failure as a dead end, while others see it as a signal to try harder, seek support, or find a better strategy. How you define failure will shape your chances of success. By reframing failure as a learning tool, you open up more paths to success.

- Vata types: Tend to adapt quickly but might change strategies too soon. For Vatas, the key is to focus on sticking to one approach long enough to see results.

- Pitta types: Are driven to succeed but can be overly self-critical. Pittas benefit from shifting their focus from results to the process, changing their perspective from "competing to win" to "competing to learn."

- Kapha types: Prefer stability and can be reluctant to change even when it's needed. For Kaphas, a supportive partner can help transition to a new strategy.

Changing Your Environment: Aligning Your Space with Your Growth Mindset

Creating a positive environment is crucial for habit success. Sometimes, our surroundings influence us more than willpower or motivation. Here's how you can modify your environment to support a growth mindset:

Visual Cues and Decluttering

- Make positive cues visible: If you want to drink more water, place water bottles in places you frequently visit, like your desk or kitchen counter. If you want to read more, keep a book on your nightstand.

- Make negative cues invisible: If you want to eat fewer cookies, hide the cookies. If you want to watch less TV, hide the TV in a cupboard that is hard to open.

- Declutter your space: Messy environments can feel like stagnant energy, making it harder to adopt new habits. As Marie Kondo suggests in her book *The Life-Changing Magic of Tidying Up*, tidying your space can improve focus and productivity. Andrew found that organizing his workspace reduced distractions and made it easier to concentrate on his design work.

Improving Your Inner Environment

While external changes are important, it's equally vital to declutter your mind. We often clutter our minds with unfinished projects or unresolved issues, which drain mental energy. Practices like meditation, nature walks, or spending time with friends can clear mental clutter, leaving you more focused and energized. Andrew started using a simple breathing technique for five minutes daily, which helped him manage stress and approach challenges more calmly.

Using Ayurveda to Promote a Growth Mindset

Ayurveda, the ancient system of holistic health, can help create environments that support your mind-body type and foster a growth mindset. Colors and aromas can have an influence in increasing or decreasing our Vata, Pitta, or Kapha. The recommendations below are to decrease or balance them.

Balancing with Colors

- Vata: Warm, soft, and pastel colors that ground Vata energy, such as green, red, orange, yellow, and gold.

- Pitta: Cooling, pale, and mild colors to keep Pitta calm, like blue, white, silver, and neutrals.

- Kapha: Bright, stimulating colors that energize Kapha energy, such as bright red, orange, and yellow.

Andrew, a Pitta type, added blue and white accents to his workspace to create a cooling and calming effect, helping him manage stress during intense design projects.

Balancing with Aromas

- Vata: Favor earthy, grounding, and sweet oils like ginger, citrus, fennel, and lavender.

- Pitta: Use soothing and cooling oils such as peppermint, sandalwood, rose, or jasmine. Andrew found that using sandalwood essential oil during meditation helped balance his fiery Pitta energy.

- Kapha: Stimulating and uplifting oils like grapefruit, bergamot, and rosemary can invigorate Kapha types.

Conclusion: Embrace Growth, Embrace Change

Andrew's journey from a fixed mindset to a growth mindset shows that lasting change is possible when you embrace challenges as learning opportunities. By applying strategies like shifting into learning, minding the gap, and wearing new shoes, Andrew was able to approach both his work and personal habits with a sense of curiosity rather than fear.

A growth mindset allows you to see failures as stepping stones rather than roadblocks. It invites you to experiment, learn, adapt, and try again, making progress an ongoing process rather than a final destination. By aligning your environment, using Ayurvedic principles, and adopting a more flexible perspective, you can achieve greater success in your personal growth journey.

As you continue with the SuperHabits approach, remember that the growth mindset isn't just a tool—it's a way of life that transforms how you face every challenge. Keep experimenting, keep learning, and keep growing.

CHAPTER 8

THE POWER OF SOCIAL SUPPORT IN HABIT CHANGE

Surround yourself only with people

who are going to lift you higher.

– Oprah Winfrey

In the quest for personal transformation, particularly in habit change, the role of social support cannot be overstated. The ancient wisdom of Ayurveda emphasizes the significance of harmonious living, not only with our physical environment but also in our relationships. This chapter explores how having an accountability partner and being part of a learning circle can profoundly influence habit change. We will also examine modern research that underscores the effectiveness of social support in overcoming challenges like smoking cessation and adopting healthier lifestyles.

A Personal Story:
Maria's experience with social support

Maria, a 52-year-old nurse, had struggled for years to establish a consistent exercise routine. Her job was demanding, with long hours and high stress, which often left her feeling exhausted by the end of the day. She had attempted numerous fitness programs but found it difficult to stick with any of them. Maria often blamed herself for lacking discipline, but the real issue was that she lacked support.

When Maria joined the SuperHabits program, she was introduced to the idea of having an accountability partner and joining a learning circle. She was initially skeptical about how much difference it could make, but decided to give it a try. Her accountability partner, Janet, was also working to establish a regular exercise habit. The two connected instantly, sharing stories of their struggles and motivating each other to keep moving forward. They set up a schedule for daily check-ins, where they would share updates, celebrate small wins, and offer encouragement during tough days. In addition to having Janet as an accountability partner, Maria also joined a learning circle that met weekly. The circle was composed of individuals focused on various habit changes, from diet improvements to yoga practices. The support she received from the group was transformative. Maria found herself more committed than ever before—her motivation wasn't just coming from within, but also from the shared success of others.

Maria's story illustrates how powerful social support can be in overcoming personal barriers. Having others to lean on made the journey less daunting and more enjoyable, helping her establish a sustainable exercise routine for the first time in years.

The Ayurvedic Perspective on Social Interactions

Ayurveda, the ancient Indian system of holistic healing, emphasizes the interconnectedness of body, mind, and spirit. It views health as a state of balance and harmony, not only within ourselves but also with our surroundings, including our relationships. Ayurveda highlights the importance of being in satsang, or the "company of truth," which means associating with people who inspire and support us in living a balanced life. Engaging with a supportive community helps reinforce positive behaviors and provides a buffer against negative influences.

In Ayurveda, the quality of our social interactions can significantly impact our mental and physical well-being. Social interactions that are positive and uplifting are considered to be nourishing, while those that are negative or stressful can disturb our inner balance. This principle applies directly to habit change: surrounding ourselves with supportive individuals can be a cornerstone in building new habits, as it provides both practical and emotional reinforcement.

The Role of an Accountability Partner

An accountability partner serves as a dedicated companion in the journey of personal growth and habit change. This individual shares a common interest in improving themselves and supports others in doing the same. The role of an accountability partner is multifaceted, encompassing motivation, feedback, and emotional reinforcement.

Benefits of an Accountability Partner

- Consistency and commitment: An accountability partner helps maintain consistent effort toward habit change. The knowledge that someone cares and is monitoring your progress encourages adherence to goals, providing external motivation that is particularly helpful during moments of weakness or self-doubt. Maria found that knowing Janet was counting on her to report back increased her commitment to exercise.

- Objective feedback: Accountability partners offer objective feedback that helps identify and address blind spots. Their perspective can provide clarity, enabling you to refine your strategies for change. Maria's partner, Janet, noticed that Maria tended to skip workouts when work stress was high. This observation prompted Maria to try shorter, stress-relief exercises during particularly tough weeks.

- Emotional support: Habit change can be emotionally taxing, and an accountability partner provides a safe space to express frustration, anxiety, or doubt. This emotional support is invaluable, as it reassures you that you're not alone in your struggles. Maria found it comforting to share her feelings of exhaustion with Janet, who understood and offered empathy, keeping her motivated even on challenging days.

- Celebration of successes: Recognizing and celebrating small victories is crucial in the process of habit change. An accountability partner helps acknowledge these successes, which boosts morale and reinforces positive behavior. Janet made a point of celebrating each week that Maria completed her exercise goals, which created a positive feedback loop.

Modern Research on Accountability Partners and Groups

Scientific research corroborates the effectiveness of accountability partners and groups in behavior change. Studies demonstrated that partners and groups improved adherence to exercise and dietary plans. Research shows that group support is more effective in smoking cessation and there is a wealth of research on the value of groups in helping with alcohol and drug abuse. A systematic review published in the *Journal of Substance Abuse Treatment* analyzed 33 studies on group therapy for substance use disorders. The findings indicated that group therapy had a significant, albeit small, effect on abstinence compared to individual therapy, suggesting that group therapy may be slightly more effective in achieving abstinence.

Additionally, a review in *Substance Abuse Treatment, Prevention, and Policy* highlighted that cognitive-behavioral therapy (CBT) and contingency management (CM) group therapies were more effective at reducing cocaine use than treatment as usual. CM also appeared effective in reducing methamphetamine use relative to standard group treatment.

Peer support groups, such as Alcoholics Anonymous (AA) and Narcotics Anonymous (NA), play a significant role in recovery. A Cochrane review found that participation in AA resulted in more individuals achieving abstinence for longer periods compared to other interventions like cognitive-behavioral therapy.

The presence of social support helps manage stress and provides motivation, which are critical factors in overcoming addiction and enacting behavior change.

The Learning Circle

A learning circle in the SuperHabits program typically comprises five to seven individuals committed to personal growth and working toward similar goals. This group-based approach provides diverse perspectives, experiences, and resources, enriching the habit-change journey.

Benefits of a Learning Circle

- Shared wisdom and resources: A learning circle brings together individuals with varied knowledge and experiences. Members share strategies, tools, and insights, helping overcome common challenges. In Maria's circle, one member shared a helpful app for tracking workouts, which Maria started using to keep herself accountable.

- Accountability and motivation: The group setting fosters natural accountability. Knowing that others are aware of your commitments can increase motivation to stay on track. This shared responsibility drives individuals to perform better and maintain consistency in their efforts. Maria felt more committed to her exercise routine because she knew she would be sharing her progress with the group.

- Encouragement and support: A learning circle offers a supportive environment where members can encourage and uplift each other. This sense of community can be a powerful motivator, helping members push through obstacles. When Maria felt discouraged, the group's support kept her spirits high.

- Diverse skill sets and talents: Each member brings unique strengths and talents to the group. This diversity fosters innovative problem-solving and provides a well-rounded support system. For instance, one member in Maria's circle was a yoga instructor who shared simple stretches that helped Maria manage back pain.

- Celebration of collective success: Celebrating achievements as a group enhances the sense of community. The collective success reinforces individual efforts, creating a positive feedback loop that encourages continued progress. Maria's group celebrated her first full month of consistent workouts, which motivated her to set even higher goals.

Implementing Social Support in Habit Change

To effectively harness social support in habit change, it's essential to thoughtfully select both an accountability partner and a learning circle. Here are practical steps to guide this process:

- Choosing an accountability partner: Select someone trustworthy, supportive, and genuinely invested in your growth. Establish clear expectations and maintain open communication through regular check-ins.

- Forming a learning circle: Gather a group of 5 to 7 individuals committed to personal growth and similar goals. Regular meetings, either in person or virtually, foster accountability, resource sharing, and mutual support. Ensure the group values confidentiality and respect.

- Creating a safe and respectful environment: In both one-on-one interactions and group settings, foster a safe space for sharing experiences and challenges. Encouraging open dialogue and empathetic listening enhances the effectiveness of social support.

- Setting clear goals and monitoring progress: Define specific, measurable goals and track progress regularly. This framework not only helps maintain focus but also provides opportunities to celebrate successes and identify areas for improvement.

- Practicing patience and compassion: Habit change is gradual and often involves setbacks. Approach this journey with patience and compassion, both for yourself and others.

Conclusion: The Transformative Power of Social Support

The journey of habit change often requires a blend of self-discipline, motivation, and perseverance. Social support, whether from an accountability partner or a learning circle, provides the structure, encouragement, and inspiration needed for lasting change. Ayurveda teaches us that we are inherently social beings, and our connections with others are integral to our well-being.

By embracing social support, the often solitary journey of habit change becomes a shared adventure. This collective journey fosters strength, resilience, and joy, helping you overcome challenges, celebrate successes, and cultivate habits that lead to a balanced and fulfilling life. As modern research confirms, social support is a critical factor in achieving and maintaining positive behavior changes. Draw upon the strength of your relationships, knowing that you are not alone in your endeavors.

With the support of others, profound and lasting transformations are possible, enriching your well-being and overall quality of life.

CHAPTER 9

THE POWER OF MEASURING YOUR SUCCESS

"Once you start tracking your goals,

you're able to see the small,

day-by-day progress that you

might not otherwise notice."

– Betsy Ramser Jaime

The journey of habit change is a complex and multifaceted process that involves setting goals, making adjustments, and persisting through challenges. One of the most critical components of this journey is the ability to measure your outcomes. Measurement is the cornerstone of effective habit change, providing the data and insights needed to evaluate progress, identify obstacles, and refine strategies. It enables you to track your progress, celebrate your achievements, and stay motivated. Without measurement, it's easy to lose sight of your goals and become disheartened by setbacks. By consistently measuring your outcomes, you create a clear picture of your journey, allowing you to make informed decisions and adjustments.

A Personal Story: Laura's journey of weight loss through measurement

Laura, a 45-year-old accountant and mother of two, had struggled with maintaining a healthy weight for most of her adult life. She had tried numerous diets and exercise plans, but without any consistent success. Laura's main challenge was not a lack of motivation; it was the absence of clear measurements. She would often start with enthusiasm but quickly lose track of her progress, leading to frustration and ultimately abandonment of her goals.

Things took a positive turn when Laura joined the SuperHabits program. The program emphasized the importance of measurement in achieving habit change, and Laura began using a simple tracking tool to monitor her food intake, exercise routines, and overall well-being. Each day, she recorded her meals, noting not only the calories but also the nutritional quality of the food. She also tracked her steps and workout routines using a fitness app that provided daily reminders and progress reports.

Within a month, Laura began noticing patterns in her behavior. For example, she realized she often snacked late at night, which contributed to her weight gain. With this awareness, she adjusted her eating habits, opting for healthier snacks earlier in the evening. The act of measuring made her more aware of her choices, and the daily tracking kept her accountable. As she saw the numbers shift on the scale, Laura felt motivated to continue, eventually losing 20 pounds over six months.

Laura's story highlights the transformative power of measurement. By consistently tracking her progress, she gained the clarity and focus needed to make meaningful changes. Her journey emphasizes that measuring outcomes isn't just about collecting data—it's about creating a sense of direction, accountability, and motivation.

The Role of Measurement in Habit Change

Research Supporting the Importance of Measurement

Research underscores the importance of measurement in behavior change. For example, a comprehensive study found that individuals who monitored their diet and physical activity were more successful in losing weight compared to those who did not track their behaviors. This finding highlights the transformative impact of self-monitoring on achieving personal goals.

Additional studies on behavior change, such as smoking cessation, have shown that individuals who monitor their smoking habits and triggers are more successful in quitting. Self-monitoring, combined with behavioral interventions, led to higher quit rates among smokers.

The Benefits of Measuring Specific Outcomes

- Clarity and focus: Measurement brings clarity and focus to your habit change efforts. By setting specific metrics, you can concentrate on what matters most and avoid distractions. Clear metrics provide a roadmap, guiding you toward your goals with precision. Laura's clear metrics for food intake and exercise helped her focus on healthier choices and more effective workout routines.

- Motivation and accountability: Regularly measuring your outcomes keeps you motivated and accountable. Seeing tangible progress reinforces your commitment and encourages you to continue. Additionally, sharing your measurements with an accountability partner or support group can provide external motivation. Laura shared her progress with her learning circle, which kept her motivated to maintain her new habits.

- Identifying patterns and trends: Measurement allows you to identify patterns and trends in your behavior. By analyzing your data, you can recognize what strategies are working and what areas need improvement. This insight enables you to make informed adjustments and optimize your approach. Laura's tracking revealed her tendency to snack at night, which she then addressed by altering her eating schedule.

- Celebrating successes: Celebrating small victories is crucial for maintaining motivation. Measurement provides the evidence needed to recognize and celebrate achievements, no matter how small. These celebrations reinforce positive behavior and build momentum. Laura celebrated each milestone, such as losing the first five pounds, which fueled her determination to continue.

- Making data-driven decisions: Data-driven decision-making is a hallmark of successful habit change. By relying on accurate measurements, you can make informed decisions about your strategies and goals.

This approach reduces guesswork and increases the likelihood of success. When Laura noticed that her weight loss had plateaued, she adjusted her workout intensity and saw immediate improvements.

Overcoming Challenges in Measuring Outcomes

While measurement is powerful, it comes with its own set of challenges:

- Maintaining consistency: Consistent measurement is crucial for accurate tracking. It can be challenging to maintain, but establishing a routine helps. Laura made it a habit to record her progress each evening before bed. Set specific times for tracking your progress each day and stick to them.

- Avoiding overwhelm: Too much data can be overwhelming. Focus on measuring key metrics that align with your goals. For example, if you're aiming to improve your diet, focus on tracking your daily intake of fruits and vegetables rather than every single food item. Simplifying the process makes measurement more sustainable.

- Interpreting data: Understanding and interpreting data is essential. Regularly review your measurements, looking for patterns and trends that can inform your next steps. If needed, seek guidance from a coach or mentor to help interpret your data effectively. Laura's learning circle offered helpful feedback on her progress, enabling her to make meaningful adjustments.

- Dealing with setbacks: Measurement can sometimes reveal setbacks, which may feel discouraging. It's important to approach these setbacks with a growth mindset, viewing them as opportunities to learn and adjust. Laura experienced a setback when she regained a few pounds after a vacation. Instead of giving up, she used the data to understand where she deviated from her routine and got back on track.

Integrating Measurement with Responsibility

Measurement and responsibility go hand in hand. By measuring your outcomes, you take ownership of your habit change journey. This integration of measurement with responsibility fosters a proactive mindset, empowering you to take control of your actions and outcomes.

THE POWER OF MEASURING YOUR SUCCESS

Practical Tools for Integrating Measurement and Responsibility

- Set personal accountability goals: Align your goals with your measurements. For example, if you are tracking your exercise routine, set a goal to share your progress with a friend or coach weekly. This external accountability reinforces commitment.

- Regular reflection: Regularly reflect on your progress and take responsibility for your actions. Use a journal to document your measurements, successes, and areas for improvement. This reflective practice enhances self-awareness and fosters a growth mindset.

- Make adjustments proactively: Use your measurements to adjust strategies. If you notice that a particular approach is not yielding the desired results, take responsibility and make necessary changes. For example, if you're tracking your steps and notice a decline, find creative ways to increase your daily movement.

Applying Christopher Avery's Responsibility Process

Christopher Avery, an expert in the field of responsibility and leadership, provides profound insights into what it means to be responsible. Avery's Responsibility Process outlines a mental model that individuals go through when dealing with problems or challenges:

- Lay blame: At this initial stage, individuals tend to blame others or external circumstances for their problems. Recognizing this tendency is the first step toward taking responsibility.

- Justify: This stage involves rationalizing failures or challenges. Overcoming this stage requires questioning whether the justifications are valid or if there are ways to work around them.

- Shame: Shame involves self-blame and guilt, which can be paralyzing. Instead of dwelling in shame, use it as a signal to reassess and adjust your approach.

- Obligation: Doing something out of obligation often leads to resentment. Find intrinsic motivation by reflecting on the deeper reasons behind your habit change.

- Responsibility: The final stage is about taking full ownership of your situation. Recognize that you have the power to change your habits and outcomes.

By applying Avery's Responsibility Process, you can reframe your approach to habit change, shifting from blame and justification to ownership and proactive adjustment. Laura learned to take responsibility for her setbacks, viewing them as opportunities to refine her approach.

Responsibility Process

Lay Blame
⇩
Justify
⇩
Shame
⇩
Obligation
⇩
Responsibility

Integrating Ayurveda for Personalized Measurement

Ayurveda offers valuable insights for personalizing measurement strategies based on your unique mind-body type:

- Vata individuals benefit from stability and routine. Focus on establishing consistent measurement practices. Use a tracking sheet to monitor regular mealtimes, hydration, and sleep patterns.

- Pitta individuals thrive on achievement and progress. Set clear, measurable goals that can be tracked consistently. Include metrics that emphasize balance, such as monitoring sleep quality and cooling foods.

- Kapha individuals may need extra stimulation to stay motivated. Use dynamic tools like habit-tracking apps with reminders. Measure progress in areas like daily movement, dietary variety, and energy levels.

Measurement is not just about numbers—it's about awareness, responsibility, and sustained growth. With a proactive, data-driven approach, you can achieve meaningful and lasting habit change. Let measurement be your compass, guiding you toward a future where your goals align with your actions and success becomes a natural outcome of your efforts.

Conclusion: The Power of Measuring for Success

Tracking your progress is key to successful habit change. It brings clarity, keeps you motivated, and holds you accountable. By consistently tracking, you can spot patterns, tackle challenges, and celebrate your achievements, all of which lead to meaningful progress. Self-monitoring is a powerful tool for long-term success, helping you stay consistent and avoid feeling overwhelmed. Combining tracking with personal responsibility and tailored approaches, like those inspired by Ayurveda, allows you to align your actions with your goals and achieve lasting results.

CHAPTER 10

YOUR FUTURE YOU

You are not just the wave, you are the ocean.

– Dr Tony Nader

What would it take to be your best possible self—to be healthier, happier, and make choices that allow you to function at your highest level in every aspect of your life? Habit change is a means of understanding yourself better and guiding your journey toward lasting transformation.

The Value of a Consciousness-Based Approach

Consciousness is the foundation of transformation, offering a pathway to meaningful and lasting habit change. While modern neuroscience explains consciousness as the result of neural activity in the brain, ancient Vedic traditions recognize it as the source of all creation and the essence of who we are. The SuperHabits approach integrates these perspectives, showing how contacting deeper levels of consciousness can dissolve inner resistance, align actions with our deeper self, and create habits that are both natural and sustainable.

Consciousness-based approaches address more than just surface behaviors—they allow us to dive below the waves of everyday thoughts and access the silent depths of the mind. Techniques like Transcendental Meditation (TM) create a direct connection to pure consciousness, the source of creativity, energy, and intelligence. This not only reduces stress but also rewires the brain, fostering mental clarity, emotional balance, and intrinsic motivation. By accessing these deeper levels of the mind, individuals gain the ability to overcome subconscious barriers and make meaningful changes with greater ease.

Contacting the deeper levels of consciousness is essential for true transformation. At these depths, where pure consciousness resides, we discover our true nature—a state of bliss, calm, and limitless potential. This direct experience of pure consciousness provides the foundation for sustained habit change. Unlike superficial approaches that rely on willpower alone, the SuperHabits approach taps into this profound source of energy and intelligence, making the process of adopting new habits more natural and aligned with the best version of ourselves.

The importance of accessing these deeper levels cannot be overstated. Many of the challenges we face when trying to change habits stem from subconscious stresses that block our progress. These stresses act like layers of pollution in the ocean of the mind, preventing us from reaching the calm depths where transformation becomes effortless. By using consciousness-based tools, we can dissolve these layers, restoring the natural flow of creativity and motivation. This process not only facilitates habit change but also enhances overall well-being, unlocking a sense of inner peace and fulfillment.

Group dynamics play a critical role in the transformation process. The concept of collective consciousness, rooted in Vedic wisdom, highlights how individuals can support each other in accessing deeper levels of consciousness. Through accountability partners and learning circles, the SuperHabits program fosters a sense of community, amplifying individual efforts and creating an environment of mutual growth.

Ultimately, the journey into consciousness is about more than adopting new behaviors; it is about reconnecting with the essence of who we are. True motivation comes from this profound connection, shifting the internal dialogue from "I have to" to "I want to." This shift creates a positive feedback loop, where each success reinforces our sense of self and builds momentum for further growth.

The SuperHabits approach reveals that habit change is not just a process of discipline but a profound exploration of consciousness. By contacting deeper levels of the mind, we unlock the potential for genuine transformation, allowing us to create a life that reflects our highest aspirations. In the silent depths of pure consciousness, we find the source of creativity, resilience, and joy—empowering us to become the best version of ourselves. Through this journey, habit change becomes more than a goal; it becomes a pathway to self-discovery, inner fulfillment, and lasting transformation.

The Value of a Personalized Approach

Every individual is unique, shaped by a complex interplay of genetics, environment, and life experiences. This individuality extends to how we approach and adopt new habits. While some people can establish routines quickly and maintain them effortlessly, others may struggle with consistency or lose motivation over time. Recognizing this diversity is essential, and the SuperHabits approach provides a solution by tailoring habit-change strategies to each individual's unique tendencies, drawing on both ancient wisdom and modern science.

The concept of "nature versus nurture" highlights the dual forces that shape us. While our genetic blueprint influences many aspects of our personality and behavior, external factors such as relationships, environment, diet, and even thoughts can modify how our genes express themselves—a phenomenon known as epigenetics. This interplay underscores the importance of a personalized approach to habit change. Effective transformation requires strategies that honor both our innate tendencies and our lived experiences.

The SuperHabits approach incorporates Ayurveda, a 5,000-year-old holistic healthcare system, to create a personalized framework for habit change. Ayurveda emphasizes balance and identifies three primary mind-body types, or doshas: Vata, Pitta, and Kapha. These doshas influence our physical, emotional, and mental characteristics, as well as how we approach change. For example, Vata types thrive on variety and creative expression

116

but may struggle with consistency. Pitta types are driven and goal-oriented but can become impatient or perfectionistic. Kapha types are steady and loyal but may require a push to overcome inertia. By understanding these dosha tendencies, the SuperHabits approach aligns habit-change strategies with an individual's natural rhythms, making the process more intuitive and sustainable.

Personalization goes beyond recognizing differences; it celebrates them. By acknowledging each individual's unique strengths and challenges, the SuperHabits approach helps people build habits that resonate with their true nature. For instance, Vata types benefit from incorporating variety and spontaneity into their routines, while Pitta types thrive with clear goals and a balance of work and relaxation. Kapha types excel with social support and structured yet gradual changes. This customized approach not only increases the likelihood of success but also fosters self-awareness and self-compassion, transforming the habit-change journey into an empowering process of self-discovery.

The SuperHabits approach demonstrates that there is no one-size-fits-all solution to habit change. By combining the timeless insights of Ayurveda with modern science, it offers a personalized, adaptable framework that respects individuality while guiding participants toward balance and fulfillment. This tailored approach helps individuals align their habits with their deeper nature, creating a foundation for lasting change and holistic well-being.

The SuperHabits Toolkit:
Practical Tools for Lasting Change

The journey to meaningful habit change requires not just intention but also effective tools to support and sustain progress. The SuperHabits Toolkit provides a comprehensive set of resources designed to address the various dimensions of habit formation— mental, emotional, and social. These tools work synergistically to help individuals create, maintain, and refine habits aligned with their deeper goals and natural tendencies. By integrating personalized strategies, emotional support, and practical systems, the Toolkit empowers participants to turn new behaviors into lasting transformations.

Habit Map: Your Roadmap to Success

The Habit Map is a cornerstone of the SuperHabits Toolkit. It provides a structured framework to help you adopt and track new habits effectively. By breaking down the process into manageable steps, the Habit Map ensures clarity and focus. It begins with defining the habit you want to establish, identifying triggers, and setting clear goals. Each step is mapped out to highlight progress and pinpoint challenges, making it easier to stay on track.

What sets the Habit Map apart is its adaptability. Whether you're building a new habit or replacing an old one, the tool allows for adjustments based on your unique circumstances and responses. By visually tracking your progress, you gain a sense of accomplishment and are better equipped to address obstacles. The Habit Map transforms habit change from an

118

abstract goal into a clear and actionable plan, giving you confidence and momentum as you move forward.

Social Support System: Strength in Community

Habit change often thrives in the presence of a supportive community, and the SuperHabits approach emphasizes the power of social connections. The Toolkit includes a social support system, featuring accountability partners and learning circles. Accountability partners provide one-on-one encouragement, helping you stay committed to your goals. They act as a mirror, reflecting your progress and helping you identify areas for improvement.

Learning circles, on the other hand, offer a group dynamic that fosters collective motivation. Sharing experiences, challenges, and victories with like-minded individuals creates a sense of camaraderie and mutual growth. This system recognizes that habit change is not an isolated journey; the energy of a supportive network can amplify individual efforts, making progress more consistent and rewarding.

Micro Habits: Small Steps, Big Results

Change doesn't have to be overwhelming. Micro Habits, another key element of the Toolkit, focus on creating small, personalized habits that are easy to implement and sustain. These bite-sized changes help build momentum without triggering resistance. For example, instead of committing to an hour-long workout, a micro habit might involve starting with five minutes of stretching each morning.

Micro Habits are especially effective for maintaining balance and focus. Their simplicity reduces the likelihood of burnout or discouragement, while their cumulative impact over time can lead to significant transformations. By keeping the focus on manageable actions, the SuperHabits Toolkit helps participants stay consistent and build confidence in their ability to create lasting change.

Tools for Emotional Balance: Navigating Inner Challenges

Emotions play a powerful role in shaping our habits, often acting as barriers or accelerators to change. The SuperHabits Toolkit includes strategies for dealing with toxic emotions and fostering emotional balance. These tools are designed to help you identify and release negative emotions such as anger, guilt, or frustration that may derail progress.

Creating an environment that supports harmonious interactions with yourself and others is central to these strategies. Practices like diaphragmatic breathing, journaling, and meditation help calm the mind and restore emotional equilibrium. By cultivating emotional balance, you create a stable foundation for habit change, reducing inner resistance and enhancing overall well-being.

Positive Affirmations: The Power of Self-Talk

Our inner dialogue has a profound impact on our ability to change. The Toolkit includes positive affirmations, which transform self-talk from inner criticism to inner coaching. These affirmations are carefully designed statements that reinforce a growth mindset, helping you overcome doubts and build self-confidence.

Instead of focusing on what you can't do, affirmations encourage a focus on possibilities and progress. For example, replacing "I always fail at this" with "I am capable of change, and I'm improving every day" rewires the mind for success. By repeating affirmations regularly, you align your thoughts with your goals, making it easier to stay motivated and resilient in the face of challenges.

Integrating the Toolkit for Holistic Habit Change

The SuperHabits Toolkit provides an integrated approach to habit change, addressing the mental, emotional, and social dimensions of the process. Each tool plays a unique role, from the structured guidance of the Habit Map to the emotional resilience fostered by meditation, affirmations and breathing techniques. Together, they create a comprehensive support system that empowers you to take small, consistent steps toward meaningful transformation.

By combining ancient wisdom with modern strategies, the Toolkit not only helps you build habits but also enhances your overall well-being. With the right tools in place, habit change becomes less about willpower and more about creating a supportive environment where new behaviors can thrive. The SuperHabits Toolkit is your companion on the journey to lasting change, helping you turn your aspirations into reality with clarity, balance, and confidence.

Conclusion: Create The Life You Want

Within you lies a unique and powerful SuperYou waiting to be uncovered. The SuperHabits approach is designed to help you unleash that power to cultivate the habits you want and create the life you deserve, from the inside out.

The best part? You can't go wrong. Just take the first step. Make a small improvement; if it works, build on it. If it doesn't, learn from it. Every step forward is progress. One step at a time, you can create the life you want.

ABOUT THE AUTHORS

DR. TONY NADER

Dr. Tony Nader, M.D., Ph.D., is a medical doctor trained at Harvard University and Massachusetts Institute of Technology (Ph.D. in neuroscience), and a globally recognized Vedic scholar.

As Maharishi Mahesh Yogi's successor, Dr. Nader is head of the international Transcendental Meditation organizations in over 100 countries. He guides the practical applications of this consciousness-based technology in all areas of national life–education, health, business, defense, agriculture, and more.

Dr. Nader's vision is to bring happiness, health, and peace to the minds and hearts of the whole world family. His experiences as a teacher, father, leader, scientist, and doctor have inspired his dedication and commitment to opening everyone's awareness to the important things in life, from a truly profound perspective. To help remove conflicts in society, so that higher values and beautiful goals become the guiding light of everyone, is his total focus.

DR. ROBERT KEITH WALLACE

Dr. Robert Keith Wallace, PhD carried out pioneering research on the Transcendental Meditation technique. His seminal papers—published in *Science*, *American Journal of Physiology*, and *Scientific American*—on a fourth major state of consciousness support a new paradigm of mind-body medicine and total brain development. Dr. Wallace is the founding President of Maharishi International University, has traveled around the world giving lectures at major universities and institutes, and has written and co-authored many books.

He is presently a Trustee of Maharishi International University and Chairman of the Department of Physiology and Health.

MIRIAM CLAES LODGE

Miriam Claes Lodge, MBA brings a wealth of knowledge teaching human development programs at McKinsey & Company, and as a career coach, Consciousness Advisor and Transcendental Meditation teacher. She graduated top of her class with her MBA from Northwestern's Kellogg School of Management and Magna Cum Laude and Cum Laude from her Bachelors and Masters in Business Engineering from KuLeuven.

She has a deep passion for helping people reach their highest potential by combining habit change with the highest knowledge of consciousness and making the world a better place for her three children.

She is currently the co-CEO of Maharishi Foundation Technologies, which offers the SuperHabits series and a number of other programs focused on developing the full potential of the individual.

HEATHERE EVANS

Heathere Evans, MA is an ICF-certified Professional Coach, consultant, and speaker on human development and change resilience. She believes deeply in the power of personal transformation and helping leaders across all generations become their most self-aware, conscious, mindful, and evolved selves. As the CEO and founder of Pivot Coaching, Inc., Heathere designs and facilitates learning programs for government and commercial organizations like the U.S. Department of Energy, Booz Allen Hamilton, and Google. The programs are based on the latest principles and practices from the fields of coaching, human development, psychology, communications, and neuroscience.

TED WALLACE

Ted Wallace, MS is currently an Agile Coach at Principal Financial Group. He has completed two Master of Science degrees, one in Computer Science and the other in Physiology, at Maharishi International University. He is a certified Scrum Master Professional (CSM, CSPO, CSP, CTC) and a registered corporate coach (RCC) with thousands of hours of coaching sessions.

ACKNOWLEDGMENTS

Our deep appreciation goes to everyone who joined the SuperHabits program and shared their transformational journey with us. We would also like to thank Jessie Kollen, Carol Markowitz, Bob Markowitz, Howard (Chancellor) Chandler, Tony Sorhaindo, Jalal Kaiser, Sandra Crowe, Kate McCullough, and Justyna Sobkowicz, for their excellent suggestions, editing, and proofreading.

APPENDICES

APPENDIX 1

MIND-BODY STATE CHARACTERISTICS

VATA MIND-BODY STATE

Vata (V) Mind-Body State individuals are bright, good at creating new ideas and projects, and able to learn quickly. If, however, they become imbalanced, they may easily lose their energy and can become fatigued and oversensitive. They may also experience mood swings, and they will then have difficulty in following a project through to the end. The secret for a V person to maintain balance is to follow a good routine. Certain simple dietary and lifestyle changes will also greatly help to rebalance and sustain a V Energy State person.

The appetite of a V person tends to be irregular and their digestive power is strong at one time and weak at another. Everyone likes to snack, but a V benefits from eating several small but nutritious meals throughout the day, rather than three "solids." It is especially important for a V to eat in a quiet environment, away from distractions and stress. When their gut is balanced, the V digestion is quite good. When the V gut is out of balance, the individual may experience symptoms such as indigestion, gas, and constipation.

See *The Rest And Repair Diet: Heal Your Gut, Improve Your Physical and Mental Health, and Lose Weight* for details about specific dietary recommendations for your Mind-Body State.

V individuals enjoy exercise that involves moving quickly and/or gracefully, but their physiology is not suited for endurance sports. They are sprinters rather than marathoners and must be very careful to not get overtired. Activities like dancing, paddleboarding, yoga—anything that keeps them moving easily—is excellent for a V. They do well with a gentle-to-moderate, grounding, warming workout.

V Mind-Body State people frequently have a hard time going to sleep and are very susceptible to insomnia. They need to understand that they must avoid excessive stimulation before bedtime and take real steps to wind down and relax, such as having a warm bath, listening to peaceful music, and using calming aromatherapy.

PITTA MIND-BODY STATE

Pitta (P) Mind-Body State individuals tend to be well-organized and purposeful. They often possess good energy and a strong and penetrating intellect, and can be good leaders. It is no coincidence that businesspeople and athletes are frequently P individuals.

When a P is imbalanced, they may have trouble controlling their anger, or, at the very least, irritation, from time to time. They can also be impatient, difficult to interact with, and controlling. The key to a P keeping in good balance is for them to eat on time and not become overheated. It's that simple!

The defining characteristic of the P Mind-Body State is a strong digestive fire. The digestive power of all Energy States is strongest at noon, and it is best for all of them to eat their largest and heaviest meal at this time. But the P gut is programmed to produce an especially powerful appetite, so it's necessary for them to eat a good amount, on time, every day, or they will experience physical discomfort and quite possibly emotional turmoil or anger. When the P gut is balanced, digestion is highly efficient; but when it is out of balance, the person can experience hyperacidity and indigestion.

P Mind-Body State individuals are usually highly competitive, and they don't hold back. Possessing stamina and strength, they are often drawn to organized sports. They are also goal-oriented and often overdo exercise, paying the consequences later. Above all, P people need to avoid becoming overheated. Active water sports like swimming, surfing, and canoeing are all good for them. If you see somebody out parasailing, that person will almost certainly prove to be a P Mind-Body State type.

A P Mind-Body State person tends to go to sleep quickly. But when the P person goes out of balance, he or she can experience difficulty sleeping.

KAPHA MIND-BODY STATE

Kapha (K) Mind-Body State people tend to be steady and take some time to carefully consider any decision. They are not easily upset, and are often easygoing and agreeable. If they go out of balance, however, they can become stubborn and may seem to lack ambition. The key to keeping a K person in good balance is to keep them physically active and mentally stimulated.

K Mind-Body State individuals have a good, steady digestion, and it doesn't bother them to miss an occasional meal. The K Energy State person loves food, but because they have a slower metabolism, they will gain weight easily, and must be careful to eat only moderate amounts.

K individuals generally have good endurance and strength, and regular active physical exercise is necessary to keep them from becoming overweight and lethargic (i.e. couch potatoes). Running, jogging, and energetic gym workouts are all very beneficial.

K Mind-Body State individuals almost never have trouble falling asleep, but they often have a hard time getting up in the morning.

VATA PITTA or PITTA VATA MIND-BODY STATES

A VP Energy State person is similar to a PV Energy State, but in written form, whichever Mind-Body State is listed first is the one that predominates. A VP person is quick, inspiring, and full of new ideas, but at the same time is also focused and ready to complete the project. VPs can be both energetic and sensitive. One part of them is in motion, while the other is steadily goal oriented.

When VPs are in good balance, they draw energy from their P qualities. When they are out of balance, their V qualities can cause them to become over-stimulated and quickly exhausted. This duality produces a reasonably strong but variable energy.

The digestion of a VP is like their energy, good but variable, and their appetite is similar. Because their gut is partially V, they may be a discriminating eater with strong preferences, and can be hungry one minute and not interested in food the next. But because their gut is also partially P, they need ample meals to sustain physical and mental activity. The presence of P indicates that it is especially important for VP individuals to eat on time. As a combination type, they have a more balanced appetite than people with either a pure V or a pure P Mind-Body State.

When VPs are in good balance, they rarely have digestive problems. When out of balance, however, digestive issues can range from weak digestion to hyperacidity.

VP Mind-Body State people are agile and have good energy and strength. They may also tend to be graceful. VP Energy individuals do not have a problem falling asleep unless they are over-stimulated before going to bed.

VATA KAPHA or KAPHA VATA MIND-BODY STATE

This Mind-Body State is an interesting combination of opposites. The V Energy State is light and airy, while the K Energy State is heavy and earthy. This combination indicates both steadiness and enthusiasm.

When VK is in good balance, the result is good health and physical stamina. When it is out of balance, VK people are prone to frequent colds and respiratory problems. With this particular energy state, it's important to remember that an imbalance of V will always push K out of balance, so V imbalances need to be addressed as soon as possible. VKs don't do well in cold or damp weather and need to stay warm to avoid illness.

The VK combination gives rise to individuals who have a wide range of emotions. They are quick, inspiring, and full of new ideas, but at the same time they are stable, well liked, and methodical. VKs can be both grounded and sensitive. One part of them is in constant airy motion, while the other is steady and grounded.

When out of balance, a VK person tends to be spacey, withdrawn, or even depressed. They may also obsess over issues and become attached and/or anxious. It's especially good for VKs to have enjoyable social outings and to stay rested, as well as energized, in order to balance the best aspects of their mind, body, and emotions.

The digestion of a VK Mind-Body State person is virtually the same as a KV Mind-Body State person. Again, as we mentioned, the mind-body state listed first indicates which is predominant. VKs are generally strong and steady, and enjoy an occasional snack. The V part of the VK combination makes the person a grazer, with a constantly changing appetite, while their K part makes them love to eat. When they are in good balance, V and K complement each other very well. They enjoy food, but don't gain as much weight as pure K types until later in life.

When out of balance, the VK, KV digestion slows down and they become more sensitive to what they eat.

In regard to exercise, VK Mind-Body State individuals are a mixture of opposites and may be sprinters as well as endurance runners.

VK Mind-Body State individuals can fall asleep and stay asleep as long as their V Mind-Body State is balanced.

PITTA KAPHA or KAPHA PITTA MIND-BODY STATE

PK Mind-Body State people have the hot, transformative qualities of a P Mind-Body State plus the cool, stable qualities of a K Mind-Body State. If they are unable to stay in balance, however, they can boil over. PKs are generally large and strong and do well in sports. Many professional athletes are PK. They might not be the stars of the team, but they have the constitution to be very good players.

A PK tends to be strong, sturdy, content, and easygoing. Their high energy drive is steadied by their calm, easygoing nature.

Imbalances can cause impatience, anger, and lethargy. They may also become argumentative, stubborn, and withdrawn. It's very important for a PK particularly to maintain healthy family relationships and friendships in order to stay in good balance.

In the heat of the moment a PK might not think problems through completely. And if decisions backfire, they may be prone to useless regret. A PK individual will be happier and healthier, spending more time listening and less time making assumptions and running scenarios in their head.

The PK digestion and appetite is virtually the same as KP. In both cases, each of the combined energy states is strong, but P will predominate. People with a P gut have a good appetite, and strong digestion. If they have a PK gut, they will have an even stronger appetite. PKs like to eat, and generally digest easily. Because their gut is part K, however, their metabolism slows down at times and they may have a hard time digesting greasy foods. It's easy for PKs to gain a few extra pounds, but they can usually lose them without great effort.

When PKs are in good balance, they rarely have digestive problems. When out of balance, however, they must be aware of slower digestion and hyperacidity.

PKs need to exercise daily. They have excellent stamina in activity, but must remember not to get overheated. The PK or KP individual generally falls asleep easily and gets a good sound sleep.

VATA PITTA KAPHA MIND-BODY STATE or "TRI-ENERGY STATE"

This is a relatively rare mixture of the three types and, when it is in balance, shows the best qualities of each. Vata Pitta Kaphas (VPKs) are often creative, motivated, steady, and good-natured. When they are in good balance, they tend to be in tune with their body and emotions and may be intuitive. Physically strong with a moderate build, VPKs are usually in good health. They avoid most seasonal illnesses and experience only mild to moderate symptoms during each season (e.g. dry skin in the winter, some lethargy in the spring, and mild heat intolerance in the summer).

Life for a VPK becomes complicated when one or more of their three Energy States goes out of balance. It is helpful for them to learn to "check in" with themselves and be alert to when something doesn't feel right. The best advice for VPKs is to treat any imbalances in the following order:

- Start by balancing V

- Go on to balance P

- Finally address K

Keep in mind that it takes a VPK Mind-Body State person longer to come back into balance than the other Mind-Body State combinations.

The digestion and appetite of a VPK Mind-Body State person should be good since they have a stronger digestion than others.

They can eat almost any kind of food and rarely experience excessive hunger or thirst. However, because their symptoms are usually mild and somewhat veiled, it is hard to pinpoint how and when they go out of balance, so it's especially valuable for them to learn to listen to their body and use Self Pulse as a reliable indicator of their state of balance.

Possessing all three characteristics, they are capable of different types of exercise. The main thing is to not overdo it. Because of their K Mind-Body State, sleep is their friend. If they do go out of balance, it is usually the V Mind-Body State which causes a sleep problem.

MIND-BODY STATE CONCLUSION

No single Mind-Body State is better than another and each of us can rise to our full potential by staying in balance and achieving maximum levels of energy, performance, and success. For recommendations about specific Mind-Body State diets, including teas, spice mixes, and recipes, see *The Rest and Repair Diet: Heal Your Gut, Improve Your Physical and Mental Health, and Lose Weight.*

SCIENTIFIC RESEARCH ON AYURVEDA AND MIND-BODY STATES

Recent studies have shown that there is a scientific basis to Ayurveda and its evaluation of each person's Mind-Body State or Prakriti. There is a whole new field emerging called Ayurgenomics. Genetic research, for example, has shown that the Vata (V Mind-Body State), Pitta (P Mind-Body

State), and Kapha (K Mind-Body State) Prakriti each expresses a different set of genes. See scientific references 1 and 2 in the list below.

Genes in the immune response pathways, for example, were turned on or up-regulated in extreme Pittas. In Vatas, genes related to cell cycles were turned on. In Kaphas it was found that genes in the immune signaling pathways were turned on. Inflammatory genes were up-regulated in Vatas, whereas up-regulation of oxidative stress pathway genes was observed in Pittas and Kaphas. See reference 3 below. CD25 (activated B cells) and CD56 (natural killer cells) were higher in Kaphas. CYP2C19 genotypes, a family of genes that help in detoxification and metabolism of certain drugs, were turned off or down-regulated in Kapha types and turned on in Pitta types. See references 4 and 5 below.

Extreme Vata, Pitta, and Kapha individuals also have significant differences in specific physiological measurements. Again, see references 1 and 2 below. Triglycerides, total cholesterol, high low-density lipoprotein (LDL), and low high-density lipoprotein (HDL) concentrations—all common risk factors for cardiovascular disease—were reported to be higher in Kaphas compared to Vatas. Hemoglobin and red blood cell count were higher in Pittas compared to others. Serum prolactin was higher in Vata individuals. See reference 2 below. High levels of triglyceride, VLDL and LDL levels and lower levels of HDL cholesterol distinguish Kaphas from others. See reference 6 below.

Adenosine diphosphate-induced maximal platelet aggregation was the highest among Vata/Pitta types. See reference 7 below. In diabetic patients, there were significant decreases in systolic blood pressure in Vata/Pitta, Pitta/Kapha, and Vata/Kapha types after walking (isotonic exercise). The Vata/Pitta types also showed significant decreases in mean diastolic blood pressure. See reference 8 below. In terms of biochemistry, Kaphas had elevated digoxin levels, increased free radical production, and reduced scavenging, increased tryptophan catabolites and reduced tyrosine catabolites, increased glycoconjugate levels, and increased cholesterol. Pittas showed the opposite biochemical patterns. Vatas showed normal biochemical patterns. See reference 9 below.

A study of basic cardiovascular responses reported that heart rate variability and arterial blood pressure during specific postural changes, exercise, and cold pressor test did not vary with constitutional type. See reference 10 below. A more recent paper measuring cold pressor test, standing-to-lying ratio, and pupillary responses in light and dark reported that Kapha types have higher parasympathetic activity and lower sympathetic activity in terms of cardiovascular reactivity as compared to Pitta or Vata types. See reference 11 below.

A recent study also showed that predominantly Vata, Pitta, or Kapha people had a different composition of bacteria in their microbiome. See reference 12 and 13 below. Sharma and Wallace in an article entitled *Ayurveda and Epigenetics* (reference 14) have shown how the time-tested lifestyle recommendations of Ayurveda act as epigenetic regulators to create balance in the physiology. Finally, Travis and Wallace have reviewed many of these findings, and created a neurophysiological model of Vata, Pitta, and Kapha based on the functioning of different neural networks. See reference 15 below.

SELECTED REFERENCES

1. Dey S, Pahwa P. Prakriti and its associations with metabolism, chronic diseases, and genotypes: Possibilities of newborn screening and a life-time of personalized prevention. J Ayurveda Integr Med 2014;5:15-24.

2. Wallace, RK. Ayurgenomics and Modern Medicine. Medicina 2020, 56, 661.

3. Juyal RC, Negi S, Wakhode P, Bhat S, Bhat B, Thelma BK. Potential of ayurgenomics approach in complex trait research: Leads from a pilot study on rheumatoid arthritis. PLoS One. 2012;7:e45752.

4. Ghodke Y, Joshi K, Patwardhan B. Traditional medicine to modern pharmacogenomics: Ayurveda Prakriti type and CYP2C19 gene polymorphism associated with the metabolic variability. Evid Based Complement Alternat Med 2011;2011:249528.

5. Aggarwal S, Negi S, Jha P, Singh PK, Stobdan T, Pasha MA. Indian genome variation consortium. EGLN1 involvement in high-altitude adaptation revealed through genetic analysis of extreme constitution types defined in Ayurveda. Proc Natl Acad Sci 2010;107:18961-6.

6. Mahalle NP, Kulkarni MV, Pendse NM, Naik SS. Association of constitutional type of Ayurveda with cardiovascular risk factors, inflammatory markers and insulin resistance. J Ayurveda Integr Med 2012;3:150-7.

7. Bhalerao S, Deshpande T, Thatte U. Prakriti (Ayurvedic concept of constitution) and variations in Platelet aggregation. BMC Complement Altern Med 2012;12:248-56.

8. Tiwari S, Gehlot S, Tiwari SK, Singh G. Effect of walking (aerobic isotonic exercise) on physiological variants with special reference to Prameha (diabetes mellitus) as per Prakriti. Ayu 2012;33:44-9.

9. Kurup RK, Kurup PA. Hypothalamic digoxin, hemispheric chemical dominance, and the tridosha theory. Int J Neurosci 2003;113:657-81.

10. Tripathi PK, Patwardhan K, Singh G. The basic cardiovascular responses to postural changes, exercise and cold pressor test: Do they vary in accordance with the dual constitutional types of Ayurveda? Evid Based Complement Alternat Med 2011;201:251-9.

11. Rapolu SB, Kumar M, Singh G, Patwardhan K. Physiological variations in the autonomic responses may be related to the constitutional types defined in Ayurveda. J Humanitas Med 2015;5:e7.

12. Chauhan NS, Pandey R, Mondal AK, Gupta S, Verma MK, Jain S, et al. Western Indian Rural Gut Microbial Diversity in Extreme Prakriti Endo-Phenotypes Reveals Signature Microbes. Front. Microbiol. 2018; 118. doi: 10.3389/fmicb.2018.00118. eCollection 2018.

13. Wallace, RK. The Microbiome in Health and Disease from the Perspective of Modern Medicine and Ayurveda. Medicina 2020; 56, 462.

14. Sharma, H.; Wallace, RK. Ayurveda and Epigenetics. Medicina 2020; 56, 687.

15. Travis FT, Wallace RK. Dosha brain-types: A neural model of individual differences. J Ayurveda Integr Med. 2015; 6, 280-85

A P P E N D I X   2

TRANSCENDENTAL MEDITATION

The Transcendental Meditation (TM) technique is a unique, simple, and effective mental procedure. It takes about 20 minutes, twice each day, sitting comfortably with your eyes closed. It involves no belief or philosophy, no mood or lifestyle. Most people begin the technique for practical reasons, such as a desire for more energy or to decrease tension and anxiety. Over 10 million people of all ages, cultures, and religions have learned TM.

TM uses the natural tendency of the mind to spontaneously experience states of greater and greater happiness. The technique involves a real and measurable process of physiological refinement that utilizes the inherent capacity of the nervous system to refine its own functioning and unfold its full potential. During TM practice, your attention is very naturally and spontaneously drawn to quieter, more orderly states of mental activity until all mental activity is transcended, and you are left with no thoughts or sensations, only the experience of pure awareness itself. The result of the regular practice of TM is that your entire nervous system becomes rejuvenated and revitalized, and you become more successful and fulfilled in activity.

Extensive research documents the effectiveness of TM in im- proving both physical and mental health. TM produces a unique state of restful alertness (2-4) with brain wave patterns that are different from other techniques of meditation (1). The practice of this technique helps every area of life by removing stress from the nervous system. Over 600 studies at more than 200 research institutes and universities have been conducted on the Transcendental Meditation program, and more than 380 of these studies have been published in peer-reviewed journals. ["Peer-reviewed" means that scientists, whose qualifications and competencies are on a similar level of accomplishment as those of the authors of the study, have evaluated the work. This method is the gold standard of science, employed to maintain the highest standard of quality and credibility.]

The US National Institutes of Health has awarded over $25 million to study the effects of TM on health, particularly on heart disease, the #1 killer in the US. It is particularly interesting to note that researchers who conducted an important study at the Medical College of Wisconsin in Milwaukee reported that the more regularly the patients meditated, the longer their term of survival (5).

A number of important studies have shown that TM reduces high blood pressure (6). A statement from the American Heart Association concluded:

> The Transcendental Meditation technique is the only meditation practice that has been shown to lower blood pressure.
>
> Because of many negative studies or mixed results and a paucity of available trials, all other meditation techniques (including MBSR) received a 'Class III, no benefit, Level of Evidence C' recommendation. Thus, other meditation techniques are not recommended in clinical practice to lower BP at this time.
>
> Transcendental Meditation practice is recommended for consideration in treatment plans for all individuals with blood pressure > 120/80 mm Hg.
>
> Lower blood pressure through Transcendental Meditation practice is also associated with substantially reduced rates of death, heart attack, and stroke (7).

Research shows that TM practice reduces cholesterol levels (8). Studies also show that meditators exhibit an improved ability to adapt to stressful situations (9,10) and a marked decrease in levels of plasma cortisol, commonly known as the "stress hormone" (11).

Research results in various areas of health document improvements in such conditions as asthma, diabetes, metabolic syndrome, pain, alcohol and drug abuse, and mental health (12-17). In a five-year study on some 2000 individuals, researchers showed that TM meditators used medical and surgical health care services approximately one-half as often as did other insurance users. This study was conducted in cooperation with Blue Cross Blue Shield and controlled for other factors that might affect health care use, such as cost sharing, age, gender, geographic distribution, and profession. The TM subjects also showed a far lower rate of increase in health care utilization with increasing age (18).

In Québec, Canada, researchers compared the changes in physician costs for TM practitioners with those of non-practitioners over a five-year period. This study is particularly reliable because the Canadian government tracked health care costs closely for both meditators and the control group, due to Canada's national health care system. After the first year, the health care costs of the TM group decreased 11%, and after five years, their cumulative cost reduction was 28%. TM patients required fewer referrals, resulting in lower medical expenses for prescription drugs, tests, hospitalization, surgery, and other treatments (19).

Studies have documented how TM can slow and even reverse the aging process. One study showed that long-term TM meditators had a biological age roughly 12 years younger than their non-meditating counterparts (20). Researchers at Harvard University studied the effects of TM on mental health, behavioral flexibility, blood pressure, and longevity, in residents of homes for the elderly. The subjects were randomly assigned either to a no-treatment group or to one of three treatment programs: the TM program, mindfulness training, or a relaxation program. Initially, all three groups were similar on pretest measures and expectancy of benefits, yet after only three months, the TM group showed significant improvements in cognitive functioning and blood pressure compared to the control groups. Reports from the TM subjects, compared to those of the mindfulness or the relaxation subjects, indicated that the TM practitioners felt more absorbed during their practice, and better and more relaxed immediately afterward. Overall, more TM subjects found their practice to be personally valuable than members of either of the control groups (21).

The most striking finding is that TM practice not only reverses age-related declines in overall health, but also directly enhances longevity. All the members of the TM group were still alive three years after the program began, in contrast to about only half of the members of the control groups. Research on the Transcendental Meditation program clearly shows that growing old can be an opportunity for further development (22,23). Scientists have suggested that one of the ways TM may improve health and increase longevity is by changing the expression of specific beneficial genes in our DNA (24,25).

Long-term changes in brain functioning have also been correlated with decreased stress-reactivity and neuroticism, and increased self-development, intelligence, learning ability, and self-actualization (26-30). One important psychological study on TM shows a significant decrease in levels of anxiety in TM practitioners as compared to subjects practicing other relaxation techniques (31). Studies in a variety of work and business settings show significantly increased productivity and efficiency (32,33). A recent study showed marked improvements in veterans with PTSD (34).

TM is learned from a qualified TM teacher, and is taught in seven steps, usually within a week's time according to your schedule. Most of the steps take one to two hours (though some are shorter). There is also a brief but important follow-up meeting 10 days after you learn the practice, and then once a month for the first three months after your TM course. All of these meetings are included in the course fee, along with lifelong support for your meditation program, including individual meditation checking, advanced meetings, and other special events.

Although there are a number of advanced TM programs, TM is always the core technique and will continue to benefit your life whether you choose to take an advanced program or not. (For more information on how to start TM, see www.tm.org.)

SELECTED REFERENCES

1. Travis FT and Shear J. Focused attention, open monitoring and automatic self-transcending: Categories to organize meditations from Vedic, Buddhist and Chinese traditions. Consciousness and Cognition 19(4):1110-1118, 2010.

2. Wallace RK. Physiological effects of Transcendental Meditation. Science 167:1751-1754, 1970.

3. Wallace RK, et al. A wakeful hypometabolic physiologic state. American Journal of Physiology 221(3): 795-799, 1971.

4. Wallace RK. Physiological effects of the Transcendental Meditation technique: A proposed fourth major state of consciousness. Ph.D. the-sis. Physiology Department, University of California, Los Angeles, 1970.

5. Schneider RH, et al. Stress Reduction in the Secondary Prevention of Cardiovascular Disease: Randomized, Controlled Trial of Transcendental Meditation and Health Education in Blacks. Circ Cardiovasc Qual Outcomes 5:750-758, 2012.

6. Rainforth MV, et al. Stress reduction programs in patients with elevated blood pressure: a systematic review and meta-analysis. Current Hypertension Reports 9:520–528, 2007.

7. Brook RD, et al., Beyond Medications and Diet: Alternative Approaches to Lowering Blood Pressure. A Scientific Statement from the American Heart Association. Hypertension 61(6):1360-83, 2013.

8. Cooper MJ, et al. Transcendental Meditation in the management of hypercholesterolemia. Journal of Human Stress 5(4): 24–27, 1979.

9. Orme-Johnson DW and Walton KW. All approaches of preventing or reversing effects of stress are not the same. American Journal of Health Promotion 12:297-299, 1998.

10. Barnes VA, et al. Impact of Transcendental Meditation on cardio-vascular function at rest and during acute stress in adolescents with high normal blood pressure. Journal of Psychosomatic Research 51: 597-605, 2001.

11. Jevning R, et al. Adrenocortical activity during meditation. Hormonal Behavior 10(1):54-60, 1978.

12. Wilson AF, et al. Transcendental Meditation and asthma. Respiration 32:74-80, 1975.

13. Paul-Labrador M, et al. Effects of randomized controlled trial of Transcendental Meditation on components of the metabolic syndrome in subjects with coronary heart disease. Archives of Internal Medicine 166:1218-1224, 2006.

14. Royer A. The role of the Transcendental Meditation technique in promoting smoking cessation: A longitudinal study. Alcoholism Treatment Quarterly 11: 219-236, 1994.

15. Haratani T, et al. Effects of Transcendental Meditation (TM) on the mental health of industrial workers. Japanese Journal of Industrial Health 32: 656, 1990.

16. Orme-Johnson DW, et al. Neuroimaging of meditation's effect on brain reactivity to pain. NeuroReport 17(12):1359-63, 2006.

17. Alexander CN, et al. Treating and preventing alcohol, nicotine, and drug abuse through Transcendental Meditation: A review and statistical meta-analysis. Alcoholism Treatment Quarterly 11: 13-87, 1994.

18. Orme-Johnson DW, Herron RE. An Innovative Approach to Reducing Medical Care Utilization and Expenditures. American Journal of Managed Care 3: 135–144, 1997.

19. Herron RE. Can the Transcendental Meditation Program Reduce the

Medical Expenditures of Older People? A Longitudinal Cost-Re- duction Study in Canada. Journal of Social Behavior and Personality 17(1): 415–442, 2005.

20. Wallace RK, et al. The effects of the Transcendental Meditation and TM-Sidhi program on the aging process. International Journal of Neuroscience 16: 53-58, 1982.

21. Alexander CN, et al. Transcendental Meditation, mindfulness, and longevity. Journal of Personality and Social Psychology 57: 950-964, 1989.

22. Alexander CN, et al. The effects of Transcendental Meditation compared to other methods of relaxation in reducing risk factors, morbidity, and mortality. Homeostasis 35: 243-264, 1994.

23. Schneider RH, et al. Long-term effects of stress reduction on mortality in persons > 55 years of age with systemic hypertension. American Journal of Cardiology 95: 1060-1064, 2005.

24. Duraimani S, et al. Effects of Lifestyle Modification on Telomerase Gene Expression in Hypertensive Patients: A Pilot Trial of Stress Reduction and Health Education Programs in African Americans. PLOS ONE 10(11): e0142689, 2015.

25. Wenuganen S, Walton KG, Katta S, Dalgard CL, Sukumar G, Starr J, Travis FT, Wallace RK, Morehead P, Lonsdorf NK, Srivastava M, Fagan J. Transcriptomics of Long-Term Meditation Practice: Evidence for Prevention or Reversal of Stress Effects Harmful to Health. Medicina (Kaunas) 57(3): 218, 2021.

26. Chandler HM, et al. Transcendental Meditation and postconventional self-development: A 10-year longitudinal study. Journal of Social Behavior and Personality 17(1): 93–121, 2005.

27. Cranson RW, et al. Transcendental Meditation and improved performance on intelligence-related measures: A longitudinal study.

Personality and Individual Differences 12: 1105-1116, 1991.

28. So KT, and Orme-Johnson DW. Three randomized experiments on the longitudinal effects of the Transcendental Meditation technique on cognition. Intelligence 29: 419-440, 2001.

29. Tjoa A. Increased intelligence and reduced neuroticism through the Transcendental Meditation program. Gedrag: Tijdschrift voor Psychologie 3: 167-182, 1975.

30. Alexander CN, et al. Transcendental Meditation, self-actualization, and psychological health: A conceptual overview and statistical meta-analysis. Journal of Social Behavior and Personality 6: 189-247, 1991.

31. Eppley KR, et al. Differential effects of relaxation techniques on trait anxiety: A meta-analysis. Journal of Clinical Psychology 45: 957-974, 1989.

32. Alexander CN, et al. Effects of the Transcendental Meditation program on stress-reduction, health, and employee development: A prospective study in two occupational settings. Stress, Anxiety and Coping 6: 245–262, 1993.

33. Harung HS, et al. Peak performance and higher states of consciousness: A study of world-class performers. Journal of Managerial Psychology 11(4): 3–23, 1996.

34. Nidich S, et al. Non-trauma-focused meditation versus exposure therapy in veterans with post-traumatic stress disorder: a randomised controlled trial. Lancet Psychiatry 5(12):975-986, 2018.

APPENDIX 3

GROUP DYNAMICS OF CONSCIOUSNESS

Maharishi Mahesh Yogi, founder of the Transcendental Meditation technique, was the first to encourage scientific research on the concept of collective consciousness. Many scientific papers, published in peer-reviewed journals, verify the practical application of Maharishi's concepts. Many of the comments about the group dynamics of consciousness can be found in Maharishi's books.

In 1960, Maharishi predicted that one percent of a population practicing the Transcendental Meditation technique would produce measurable improvements in the quality of life for the whole population. This phenomenon was first studied in 1974 and was referred to as the "Maharishi Effect." In 1976, Maharishi brought out several advanced programs derived from the Vedic tradition, which greatly enhanced the Maharishi Effect. Scientists found that when even the square root of one percent of any population practices these programs in a group, there is a measurable marked reduction in violence and an improvement in the quality of life, a type of macroscopic field effect of coherence.

A large number of studies have documented the beneficial effects of the practice of TM and its advanced programs on reducing crime and violence and improving the quality of life in different areas of the world. One demonstration project was conducted in 1993 in Washington, DC by Dr. John Hagelin and colleagues. An independent panel of more than 20 sociologists, criminologists, and members of the Washington, DC government and police department advised on the study design and reviewed the analysis of the findings. The study included over 4000 people gathered in Washington to participate in a "peace assembly," practicing TM and specific related advanced programs for extended periods. Results showed that as the group size increased, there was a highly significant decrease in violent crime.

A remarkable aspect of this study was that it took place in the summer, when the weather is especially hot in Washington. In fact, the police chief of Washington, who sat on the independent board of researchers monitoring the project, said in an interview, "The only way this group can lower crime by 20 percent in Washington in August is if we have two feet of snow!" In fact, the meditating group lowered crime by 23.6 percent.

How could such a thing happen? The individuals in the group didn't go out on the streets and physically stop people from committing crimes. They simply meditated quietly together in various locations around the city. The coherence effect which they created in the collective consciousness of the city was similar to the result of throwing a pebble in a pond: ripples of higher, more coherent waves of consciousness went out in all directions, creating that crime was spontaneously reduced.

Research demonstrates that it is possible to influence the collective consciousness of society through the group practice of the TM technique and its advanced programs.

SELECTED REFERENCES

1. Hagelin JS, et al. Effects of group practice of the Transcendental Meditation program on preventing violent crime in Washington, DC: results of the National Demonstration Project, June-July 1993. Social Indicators Research 47: 153-201, 1999.

2. Orme-Johnson DW, et al. International peace project in the Middle East: The effect of the Maharishi Technology of the Unified Field. Journal of Conflict Resolution 32: 776–812, 1988.

3. Orme-Johnson DW, et al. The long-term effects of the Maharishi Technology of the Unified Field on the quality of life in the United States (1960 to 1983). Social Science Perspectives Journal 2:127-146, 1988.

4. Orme-Johnson DW, et al. Preventing terrorism and international conflict: Effects of large assemblies of participants in the Transcendental Meditation and TM-Sidhi programs. Journal of Offender Rehabilitation 36: 283–302, 2003.

5. Brown CL. Overcoming barriers to use of promising research among elite Middle East policy groups. Journal of Social Behavior and Personality 17:489-546, 2005.

6. Cavanaugh KL. Time series analysis of U.S. and Canadian inflation and unemployment: A test of a field-theoretic hypothesis. Proceedings of the

American Statistical Association, Business and Economics Statistics Section (Alexandria, VA: American Statistical Association): 799–804, 1987.

7. Cavanaugh KL, King KD. Simultaneous transfer function analysis of Okun's misery index: Improvements in the economic quality of life through Maharishi's Vedic Science and technology of consciousness. Proceedings of the American Statistical Association, Business and Economics Statistics Section (Alexandria, VA: American Statistical Association): 491–496, 1988.

8. Davies JL. Alleviating political violence through enhancing coherence in collective consciousness. Dissertation Abstracts International 49(8): 2381A, 1989.

9. Gelderloos P, et al. The dynamics of US–Soviet relations, 1979–1986: Effects of reducing social stress through the Transcendental Meditation and TM-Sidhi program. Proceedings of the Social Statistics Section of the American Statistical Association (Alexandria, VA: American Statistical Association): 297–302, 1990.

10. Dillbeck MC. Test of a field theory of consciousness and social change: Time series analysis of participation in the TM-Sidhi program and reduction of violent death in the U.S. Social Indicators Research 22: 399–418, 1990.

11. Assimakis PD, Dillbeck MC. Time series analysis of improved quality of life in Canada: Social change, collective consciousness, and the TM-Sidhi program. Psychological Reports 76: 1171–1193, 1995.

12. Hatchard GD, et al. A model for social improvement. Time series analysis of a phase transition to reduced crime in Merseyside.

13. Dillbeck MC, et al. The Transcendental Meditation program and crime rate change in a sample of forty-eight cities. Journal of Crime and Justice 4: 25–45, 1981.

14. Dillbeck MC, et al. Test of a field model of consciousness and social change: The Transcendental Meditation and TM-Sidhi program and decreased urban crime. The Journal of Mind and Behavior 9: 457–486, 1988.

15. Dillbeck MC. et al. Consciousness as a field: The Transcendental Meditation and TM-Sidhi program and changes in social indica- tors. The Journal of Mind and Behavior 8: 67–104, 19

APPENDIX 4

DIAPHRAGMATIC BREATHING

Diaphragmatic breathing is about putting your attention on the diaphragm and making sure it is actually participating in the breathing process.

The diaphragm is a key muscle in the body, located between the thorax and the abdominal cavity, it is the engine of our breathing. If we are only breathing with the chest muscles, the breath can become shallow, or sluggish, which is not the most effective way to breathe.

Diaphragmatic breathing helps to deepen the breath, which can help with heart, lung, and respiratory problems. Normalizing breathing also settles the mind and body, which is helpful in preparing us for pranayama and meditation.

You can follow this simple process:

Start by sitting comfortably and easily in a chair and close your eyes. Put one hand on your chest (right or left is fine)— then put the other on your abdomen.

Inhale through the nostrils— feeling your abdomen moving out. As you inhale, you will also feel the hand on your abdomen moving outwards.

1. Now exhale through your mouth, with a feeling of softly blowing on something. As you exhale, you will feel the hand on the abdomen moving in, towards your back. When you have done this 2-3 times, put your attention on your hand that is on your chest. You will feel it is not moving. It is the silent part. Do this for a few breaths, feeling that silent part.

2. Now have your attention on the softness of your hands (everything is happening with your attention). Your attention goes from one hand to the other, and in that attention, you will feel the softness, the easiness of the hands.

3. Then move to the feeling of the shoulders, as you continue to experience the inflow of air moving the abdomen outwards and the outflow of air moving the abdomen inwards.

With your attention on your shoulders, make sure they are not shrugged up or tense, that they are easy and relaxed. See that your arms are hanging from the shoulders relaxed, that everything is soft.

4. Then go to your face. Feel that your face is soft; your jaw is relaxed.

5. Then go back to your hands and do the same. Feel that your hands are soft and moving properly—this means that the hand on the abdomen is moving in and out, while the hand on the chest is settled and soft.

6. Then go back to your shoulders, and feel that they are soft, and then go to the face and jaw. Circle like this a few times, then put your hands down and slowly open your eyes, in a soft, slow way. No rushing. Take the breathing normally, as it is.

APPENDIX 5

PRANAYAMA

Pranayama, or comfortable breathing exercise, is an ancient technique that enhances vitality and promotes longevity by encouraging slow, deep, and mindful breathing. It establishes regular breathing patterns, restoring natural rhythms to the body and mind, which can improve physical and mental health. Benefits include strengthened lungs and heart, improved digestion, purified nervous system, and increased energy.

How to practice pranayama:

- Sit in a comfortable position on a chair or sofa and close your eyes.

- Breathe in through both nostrils.

- Close the right nostril with the thumb of your right hand and breathe out through the left nostril, slowly and completely.

- Breathe in through the same (left) nostril and then close the left nostril with the ring and middle finger of the right hand while opening the right nostril to breathe out. Do it noiselessly, slowly, and completely.

- Now breathe in again through the right nostril.

- Breathe out and in through the left nostril while closing the right nostril; close the left nostril and breathe out and in through the right nostril.

- Continue the same way for 4-5 minutes, at your own pace, breathing slowly, completely and comfortably.

- To finish doing Pranayama, after breathing in through the right nostril, release your hands and breathe out through both nostrils.

If at any point, the breathing exercise begins to feel uncomfortable, please do not strain to complete the full 4-5 minutes. In this case, take a momentary break and return to complete the 4-5 minutes whenever you feel ready.

Pranayama is believed to influence the autonomic nervous system, specifically the parasympathetic and sympathetic responses, which control the body's stress and relaxation states.

REFERENCES

USEFUL WEBSITES

www.superhabits.com

ww.tm.org

www.miu.edu

USEFUL REFERENCES

Introduction

Neuroadaptability and Habit: Modern Medicine and Ayurveda. Medicina 2021, 57, 90. doi: 10.3390/medicina57020090.

Chapter 1

Living in Balance with Maharishi AyurVeda: Practical Therapies for Consciousness-Based Health by Robert Keith Wallace, PhD, Karin Pirc, MD, Julia Clarke, MS, MIU Press, 2023.

Chapter 2

Consciousness Is All There Is: How Understanding and Experiencing Consciousness Will Transform Your Life by Dr. Tony Nader, Hay House, 2024.

Living in Balance with Maharishi AyurVeda: Practical Therapies for Consciousness-Based Health by Robert Keith Wallace, PhD, Karin Pirc, MD, Julia Clarke, MS, MIU Press, 2023.

Mondal, S. (2024). Proposed physiological mechanisms of pranayama: A discussion. Journal of Ayurveda and Integrative Medicine, 15(1), 100877. https://doi.org/10.1016/j.jaim.2023.100877.

Chapter 3

Living in Balance with Maharishi AyurVeda: Practical Therapies for Consciousness-Based Health by Robert Keith Wallace, PhD, Karin Pirc, MD, Julia Clarke, MS, MIU Press, 2023.

The Greater Good Magazine: Science-Based Insights for a Meaningful Life by the University of California, Berkeley, 2024.

Chapter 4

The Molecule of More: How a Single Chemical in Your Brain Drives Love, Sex, and Creativity – And Will Determine the Fate of the Human Race by Daniel Z. Lieberman MD, Michael E. Long, BenBella Books 2019.

Chapter 5

Self Empower by Robert Keith Wallace, Samantha Wallace, and Ted Wallace, Dharma Publications, 2020.

Chapter 6

Living in Balance with Maharishi AyurVeda: Practical Therapies for Consciousness-Based Health by Robert Keith Wallace, PhD, Karin Pirc, MD, Julia Clarke, MS, MIU Press, 2023.

The Rest And Repair Diet: Heal Your Gut, Improve Your Physical and Mental Health, and Lose Weight by Robert Keith Wallace, PhD, Samantha Wallace, Andrew Sternberg, MA Jim Davis, DO, and Alexis Farley, Dharma Publications, 2019.

Chapter 7

Living in Balance with Maharishi AyurVeda: Practical Therapies for Consciousness-Based Health by Robert Keith Wallace, PhD, Karin Pirc, MD, Julia Clarke, MS, MIU Press, 2023.

Mindset: The New Psychology of Success by Carol S. Dweck, Ph.D., Ballantine Books, 2007.

Authentic Success: Essential Lessons and Practices from the World's Leading Coaching Program on Success Intelligence by Robert Holden, Ph.D., Hay House, 2011.

Chapter 8

Buller DB, Borland R, Woodall WG, Hall JR, Hines JM, Burris-Woodall P, Cutter GR, Miller C, Balmford J, Starling R, Ax B, Saba L. Randomized trials on consider this, a tailored, internet-delivered smoking prevention program for adolescents. Health Educ Behav. 2008 Apr;35(2):260-81. doi: 10.1177/1090198106288982. Epub 2006 Nov 17. PMID: 17114331; PMCID: PMC4380290.

Wing RR, Jeffery RW. Benefits of recruiting participants with friends and increasing social support for weight loss and maintenance. J Consult Clin Psychol. 1999 Feb;67(1):132-8. doi: 10.1037//0022-006x.67.1.132. PMID: 10028217.

Kullgren JT, Troxel AB, Loewenstein G, Asch DA, Norton LA, Wesby L, Tao Y, Zhu J, Volpp KG. Individual- versus group-based financial incentives for weight loss: a randomized, controlled trial. Ann Intern Med. 2013 Apr 2;158(7):505-14. doi: 10.7326/0003-4819-158-7-201304020-00002. PMID: 23546562; PMCID: PMC3994977.

Harvey-Berino, J., Pintauro, S., Buzzell, P., & Gold, E. C. (2004). Effect of Internet Support on the Long-Term Maintenance of Weight Loss. Obesity Research, 12(2), 320–329. https://doi.org/10.1038/oby.2004.40.

Stead LF, Carroll AJ, Lancaster T. Group behaviour therapy programmes for smoking cessation. Cochrane Database Syst Rev. 2017 Mar 31;3(3):CD001007. doi: 10.1002/14651858.CD001007.pub3. PMID: 28361497; PMCID: PMC6464070.

Porca C, Rodriguez-Carnero G, Tejera C, Andujar P, Casanueva FF, Crujeiras AB, Bellido D. Effectiveness to promote weight loss maintenance and healthy lifestyle habits of a group educational intervention program in adults with obesity: IGOBE program. Obes Res Clin Pract. 2021 Nov-Dec;15(6):570-578. doi: 10.1016/j.orcp.2021.10.003. Epub 2021 Nov 4. PMID: 34742669.

Yorks DM, Frothingham CA, Schuenke MD. Effects of Group Fitness Classes on Stress and Quality of Life of Medical Students. J Am Osteopath Assoc. 2017 Nov 1;117(11):e17-e25. doi: 10.7556/jaoa.2017.140. PMID: 29084328.

Street S, Avenell A. Are individual or group interventions more effective for long-term weight loss in adults with obesity? A systematic review. Clin Obes. 2022 Oct;12(5):e12539. doi: 10.1111/cob.12539. Epub 2022 Jun 28. PMID: 35765718; PMCID: PMC9542282.

John, J.C., Ho, J., Raber, M. *et al.* Dyad and group-based interventions in physical activity, diet, and weight loss: a systematic review of the evidence. *J Behav Med* 47, 355–373 (2024). https://doi.org/10.1007/s10865-023-00457-z.

Lo Coco G, Melchiori F, Oieni V, Infurna MR, Strauss B, Schwartze D, Rosendahl J, Gullo S. Group treatment for substance use disorder in adults: A systematic review and meta-analysis of randomized-controlled trials. J Subst Abuse Treat. 2019 Apr;99:104-116. doi: 10.1016/j.jsat.2019.01.016. Epub 2019 Jan 24. PMID: 30797382.

López G, Orchowski LM, Reddy MK, Nargiso J, Johnson JE. A review of research-supported group treatments for drug use disorders. Subst Abuse Treat Prev Policy. 2021 Jun 21;16(1):51. doi: 10.1186/s13011-021-00371-0. PMID: 34154619; PMCID: PMC8215831.

Kelly JF, Abry A, Ferri M, Humphreys K. Alcoholics Anonymous and 12-Step Facilitation Treatments for Alcohol Use Disorder: A Distillation of a 2020 Cochrane Review for Clinicians and Policy Makers. Alcohol Alcohol. 2020 Oct 20;55(6):641-651. doi: 10.1093/alcalc/agaa050. PMID: 32628263; PMCID: PMC8060988.

Chapter 9

Burke LE, Wang J, Sevick MA. Self-monitoring in weight loss: a systematic review of the literature. J Am Diet Assoc. 2011 Jan;111(1):92-102. doi: 10.1016/j.jada.2010.10.008. PMID: 21185970; PMCID: PMC3268700.

Locke EA, Latham GP. Building a practically useful theory of goal setting and task motivation. A 35-year odyssey. Am Psychol. 2002 Sep;57(9):705-17. doi: 10.1037//0003-066x.57.9.705. PMID: 12237980.

Fang YE, Zhang Z, Wang R, Yang B, Chen C, Nisa C, Tong X, Yan LL. Effectiveness of eHealth Smoking Cessation Interventions: Systematic Review and Meta-Analysis. J Med Internet Res. 2023 Jul 28;25:e45111. doi: 10.2196/45111. Erratum in: J Med Internet Res. 2024 Feb 7;26:e56438. doi: 10.2196/56438. PMID: 37505802; PMCID: PMC10422176.

Whittaker R, McRobbie H, Bullen C, Rodgers A, Gu Y, Dobson R. Mobile phone text messaging and app-based interventions for smoking cessation. Cochrane Database Syst Rev. 2019 Oct 22;10(10):CD006611. doi: 10.1002/14651858.CD006611.pub5. PMID: 31638271; PM- CID: PMC6804292.

Bricker JB, Mull KE, Kientz JA, Vilardaga R, Mercer LD, Akioka KJ, Heffner JL. Randomized, controlled pilot trial of a smartphone app for smoking cessation using acceptance and commitment therapy. Drug Alcohol Depend. 2014 Oct 1;143:87-94. doi: 10.1016/j.drugalcdep.2014.07.006. Epub 2014 Jul 17. PMID: 25085225; PM- CID: PMC4201179.

Harkin B, Webb TL, Chang BP, Prestwich A, Conner M, Kellar I, Benn Y, Sheeran P. Does monitoring goal progress promote goal attainment? A meta-analysis of the experimental evidence. Psychol Bull. 2016 Feb;142(2):198-229. doi: 10.1037/bul0000025. Epub 2015 Oct 19. PMID: 26479070.

Zhao J, Freeman B, Li M. Can Mobile Phone Apps Influence People's Health Behavior Change? An Evidence Review. J Med Internet Res. 2016 Oct 31;18(11):e287. doi: 10.2196/jmir.5692. PMID: 27806926; PM- CID: PMC5295827.

Spreckley M, Seidell J, Halberstadt J. Perspectives into the experience of successful, substantial long-term weight-loss maintenance: a systematic review. Int J Qual Stud Health Well-being. 2021 Dec;16(1):1862481. doi: 10.1080/17482631.2020.1862481. PMID: 33455563; PM- CID: PMC7833027.

Sharma H, Wallace RK. Ayurveda and Epigenetics. Medicina (Kaunas). 2020 Dec 11;56(12):687. doi: 10.3390/medicina56120687. PMID: 33322263; PMCID: PMC7763202.

The Responsibility Process: Unlocking Your Natural Ability to Live and Lead with Power by Christopher Avery, Partnerwerks, 2016.

INDEX

A

attention, 3, 145, 151, 161, 162

Ayurgenomics, 140, 143

Ayurveda, x, xii, 4, 8, 10, 28, 36, 49, 72, 74, 90, 93, 95, 102, 111, 116, 117, 140, 142, 143, 144, 167, 168, 173

B

balance, xii, 4, 8, 11, 12, 13, 14, 15, 26, 37, 38, 73, 80, 90, 91, 95, 111, 114, 116, 117, 120, 121, 131, 133, 134, 135, 136, 137, 138, 139, 140, 143

brain wave, 146

C

collective consciousness, 27, 115, 155, 156, 157, 158

consciousness, viii, x, xiii, xiv, xviii, 16, 19, 20, 21, 22, 23, 24, 25, 26, 27, 28, 30, 41, 46, 49, 113, 114, 115, 124, 151, 154, 155, 157, 158, 159

digestion, 11, 12, 71, 72, 131, 133, 134, 135, 136, 137, 138, 139, 165

D

DNA, 8, 150

Energy State, 131, 134, 136

Energy States, 133, 139

epigenetic, 142

exercise, vii, ix, xiv, xvi, 8, 10, 14, 22, 23, 24, 34, 38, 57, 70, 74, 77, 84, 86, 94, 95, 96, 97, 99, 104, 106, 109, 132, 133, 134, 137, 138, 140, 142, 144, 165, 166

H

happiness, vii, xviii, 145

health, ii, vii, xii, xviii, 3, 4, 22, 25, 26, 28, 65, 75, 79, 80, 90, 95, 136, 139, 146, 148, 149, 152, 154, 165

K

K Energy State, 136
Kapha, xii, 5, 7, 8, 10, 13, 14, 15, 16, 28, 29, 38, 63, 64, 67, 72, 73, 74, 76, 88, 90, 91, 112, 116, 117, 134, 141, 142

M

Maharishi, ii, 3, 20, 124, 125, 126, 155, 157, 158, 167, 168, 169
meditation, xiv, xvi, xvii, 8, 13, 24, 25, 26, 33, 41, 58, 60, 63, 77, 78, 89, 91, 120, 121, 146, 147, 150, 152, 154, 161
microbiome, 142
motivation, ix, xv, 12, 13, 14, 22, 24, 25, 27, 28, 32, 34, 44, 45, 46, 47, 48, 49, 50, 51, 60, 66, 78, 79, 88, 94, 96, 98, 99, 102, 104, 105, 106, 110, 114, 115, 116, 119, 172

N

nervous system, xiv, 19, 26, 40, 145, 146, 165, 166
Neuroscience, xiii, 46, 153

P

Pitta, xii, xiv, 5, 7, 8, 10, 12, 13, 16, 28, 29, 37, 39, 63, 64, 67, 72, 73, 74, 76, 88, 90, 111, 116, 117, 132, 139, 140, 141, 142
Prakriti, 140, 143, 144

R

relationships, 4, 21, 79, 93, 95, 102, 116, 138
Rest and Repair Diet, 140

S

Self Pulse, 140
sleep, vii, 6, 11, 33, 34, 38, 71, 75, 77, 111, 132, 133, 138, 140
stress, vii, ix, xi, xii, xiii, xiv, 4, 5, 6, 7, 13, 22, 23, 24, 25, 32, 33, 34, 36, 38, 57, 58, 60, 77, 79, 86, 89, 90, 94, 96, 98, 114, 131, 141, 146, 148, 150, 151, 152, 153, 154, 158, 166

Printed in Great Britain
by Amazon